MOBILE WEB
DESIGNER'S IDEA BOOK

the ultimate guide to trends, themes and styles in mobile web design

PATRICK McNEIL, bestselling author of *The Web Designer's Idea Book* series

MOBILE WEB

DESIGNER'S IDEA BOOK

the ultimate guide to trends, themes and styles in mobile web design

HOW

For more excellent books and resources for designers, visit www.howdesign.com.

7 16 15 14 13   5 4 3 2 1

ISBN-13: 978-1-4403-3008-7

Distributed in Canada by Fraser Direct
100 Armstrong Avenue
Georgetown, Ontario, Canada L7G 5S4
Tel: (905) 877-4411

Distributed in the U.K. and Europe by F&W Media International, LTD
Brunel House, Forde Close, Newton Abbot, TQ12 4PU, UK
Tel: (+44) 1626 323200, Fax: (+44) 1626 323319
Email: enquiries@fwmedia.com

Distributed in Australia by Capricorn Link
P.O. Box 704, Windsor, NSW 2756 Australia
Tel: (02) 4560-1600

fw
media

Edited by Scott Francis
Designed by Claudean Wheeler
Production coordinated by Greg Nock

DEDICATION

For my kids, Jack and Maizy, who will never know a world without mobile devices.

ABOUT THE AUTHOR

 Patrick is a designer, developer and writer; but above all things he is a passionate educator. It is this core passion that leads him to write books, teach students and relentlessly share the knowledge and ideas he collects. Patrick began his public exploration of design on his blog DesignMeltdown.com which eventually turned into a best-selling series of books (TheWebDesignersIdeaBook.com). With inter-ests in both technology and design, he has found himself at home on the web where these two areas merge so perfectly. Beyond observing trends, he is focused on front-end development techniques and teaching designers to effectively leverage the web as a design medium. For more information about Patrick, visit his personal site, pmcneil.com, or follow him on Twitter @designmeltdown.

ACKNOWLEDGMENTS

As I have said so many times before, my books would not be possible were it not for the countless designers around the world pouring their hearts into their work. To all those designers, I say, "Thank you." Your beautiful work makes the web a beautiful place to work; it makes my job a joy, and it makes my books possible. I sincerely admire your work and appreciate your passion.

I also want to thank my many friends at F+W Media: Over and over they allow me to write books, speak at events, teach courses and generally let me do most anything I want. I am very lucky to be paired with them.

Finally, I want to thank my wife, who relentlessly supports my writing and atypical work. Her determination and insistence on pushing toward our dreams keeps me looking forward and finding ways to make books like this one a reality.

Contents

Word From the Author

I have wanted to do a book on mobile web design for a number of years now. But for a long time, the community was really focused on mobile apps and not the mobile web. And in reality, there simply weren't enough beautiful mobile websites to fill a book. In the last *few* years, though, this has changed and mobile websites now receive equal attention. Even still, it has taken a few years for the quantity of beautiful work to get large enough to make a book like this possible. For every site that makes it into this book, I looked at ten others that won't, so there really has to be a fair amount of work to select from.

Sometimes I think we forget that the first iPhone came out just a few years ago in 2007. And it took until around 2011 for the web to truly embrace mobile websites. It seems that the saturation of mobile devices, in large part spurred by the flurry of tablet sales, reached a tipping point and the mobile web simply became mission critical to the online world. In fact, it is predicted that by 2014, mobile web traffic will exceed web traffic from desktop computers. To say that the landscape of web design and development is changing is a radical understatement.

Putting this book together has been an absolute thrill and a real eye-opener. We all know that the mobile web is a hot topic and that a lot is happening. But in reality, it has completely exploded. The mobile web can be a bit harder to navigate and randomly surf, so it has actually grown far more than many of us realize. Researching this book showed me just how far-reaching it is, and hopefully through this book you'll gain some insights into areas you would never have found. Ultimately, I am thrilled with the results gathered here and I look forward to seeing how you apply the ideas in your own work.

Future Books

If you would like to submit your designs for possible use in future books, please visit thewebdesigner-sideabook.com to sign up for my mailing list. You will be informed of book releases, calls for entries and other information directly related to the books.

QR CODES

Throughout this book you will find QR codes. If you scan these codes, they will take you to landing **pages** where you can find links to all of the samples presented in any given chapter. This means you can scan the code and quickly launch and try out the sites I have selected without having to type URL into your device.

A QR code is essentially a special type of barcode. You can install a QR code scanner on your phone or tablet that will allow you to scan the tag, and it will take you to a URL. Note that many bar code scanner apps also scan QR codes. In fact, my favorite bar code scanner on my Android device scans QR codes as well: the app is creatively titled Barcode Scanner.

In time, many of these sites will change, and some will disappear altogether, but this is the nature of the web and my books are but a snapshot in time. However, I do believe the majority will remain the same and accessible for a fairly long period of time. Eventually I may update the landing pages with full size images, as presented in the book. This way, in the future, the QR codes will still serve a useful purpose.

As you read this book, keep your smartphone handy. If you see a design you like, simply scan the code and browse the live site.

ICONS

Throughout this book you will find URLs denoted with icons to indicate how the look on each type of device, as follows:
Ⓜ Mobile Ⓣ Tablet Ⓓ Desktop

01

Defining Mobile

Surprising as it may be, defining what constitutes "mobile" is actually not as simple as one might expect. In fact, it can actually be rather controversial. Consider devices like the iPad. Some people (including Mark Zuckerberg[1], for example) consider it to be a computer. Sure, you can carry it around with you, making it "mobile" to many, but at the same time, it is larger and often used as a laptop replacement, making it not so mobile-ish. Case in point: I actually wrote much of this very book on my iPad, using a Bluetooth keyboard. And somewhere near the end of writing it, I switched to my Asus Netbook—which is a laptop of course—but it's actually smaller than my iPad/keyboard combo. As I said, defining mobile is not as simple as one might think.

Another example that comes to mind is that cars will soon have built in tablet-like interfaces; will they be computers or mobile devices? It is not too hard to imagine automobiles that connect to the Internet via cell networks. And from there, imagine an iPad-like interface built right in. You can customize it, install apps, download music, etc.

---

[1] http://www.wired.com/gadgetlab/2010/11/fighting-words-defining-mobile-and-computer/

It hardly feels like a stretch to propose such an idea. So, while it might be splitting hairs, will we call such an interface "mobile"? Perhaps "on-the-go" is better.

A final example is the recent influx of Windows 8–based products that blur the lines— tablets that become laptops, desktops that become tablets, and so on. What is and isn't mobile is not very easy to pin down anymore.

The reality is that the devices people are using to browse websites are changing rapidly. I could hardly get this book written without waves of new devices being released. So while I understand that defining mobile isn't easy, I am going to put my own boundaries on the definition for the sake of establishing what I plan to focus on in this book. This book is about the mobile web; it is *not* about mobile apps. It covers design styles and patterns as they are found on websites and will not focus on apps you install to your devices.

For the purposes of this book, I will lump mobile devices into two main categories. The first category is smartphones. It should come as no surprise that this will include the iPhone. Basically any phone that qualifies as a smartphone is a candidate. And it is this interface that will be the primary focus of the book.

The second main category—the secondary focus of this book—is tablets. Tablets seem to fall into two main subsets, based on screen size: The first is around 7 inches; the second is around 10. In my experience, the smaller of these tends to feel more like a large phone, while the larger tends to feel like a small laptop. The difference is not inconsequential. I find support for this in that you often find sites rendering in a similar fashion on smartphones and 7" tablets. Meanwhile, many sites render on a 10" tablet as a slightly-minimized version of the full desktop site. Incidentally, the Samsung Note, with its 5.3-inch screen, feels like a tiny tablet as opposed to a large phone—which is what it actually is. The lines between device types are extremely fuzzy.

02

Approaches

The goal is to cater to mobile users. The means to do so vary. I will cover three primary ways to accomplish this: mobile-specific, responsive and fluid design. At the simplest level, a site either adapts in some way to the user's environment, or the user is directed to a mobile-specific version of the site. Historically speaking, most sites that wanted to address mobile used a separate URL and had a 100% mobile specific interface. We still find that this is a popular approach in certain cases. On the other hand, the whole responsive web design revolution encompasses the very simple idea of adapting the site to fit and function properly in any environment.

Before we dive in, I want to mention one thing. There are other methods that we can use, like theme-switching, where the theme for the site (the skin on top of the content) dynamically changes depending on the user's screen size. Or server-side site adjustments, where the server detects the user's environment, follows some logic, and outputs a page specifically matched to the device. While these are relevant and valuable solutions, in one form or another they easily fit under the following umbrellas.

Mobile Specific

With this approach, site owners maintain separate versions of a website. One is intended for the standard desktop user and another for mobile users (typically phone-based). This technique is popular for several reasons. First, it makes building and testing each site a bit easier. When adjustments are made to the desktop version, you are comfortable knowing that you aren't messing up the mobile version and therefore don't have to retest it as well.

One huge benefit to this approach is that you can cater the content, site structure and entire mission of the site to fit the usage of the site. This means that each can be optimized to fit the separate and unique goals of each environment. We may assume users looking at our site on a phone want the same thing as desktop user sitting in a cubicle, but is this accurate? I can think of numerous cases where I expect very different things.

A perfect demonstration of this is the 280daily website. The desktop version **(FIGURE 1)** of this site works to sell the product. It gives you information on what it does and enables you to sign up. In contrast, the mobile-specific version **(FIGURE 2)** focuses primarily on allowing you to log in and use the application. In this environment, the goals are reversed and converting new users takes the backseat.

I am a part of a conference series that uses mobile sites at the actual event. In this case, it is rather easy to see how a mobile site for the HOW Interactive Conference **(FIG-URE 3)** [addresses radically different needs than the standard desktop site **(FIGURE 4)**. The mobile version is used *at* the event while the desktop site is used to sell and promote the event before it happens. These radically different goals create a perfect situation for a mobile-specific site.

FIGURE 1: http://280daily.com

FIGURE 2: http://280daily.com/m

FIGURE 3: http://codifydesign.com/go/howidc-sf   **FIGURE 4:** www.howinteractiveconference.com

www.thegift.pt/primaveraextras/m

www.thegift.pt/primaveraextras Ⓓ

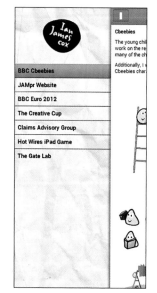

www.ianjamescox.com/m Ⓜ

www.ianjamescox.com Ⓓ

www.playtennis.com **D**

m.playtennis.com **M**

www.casulo.pt **D**

www.casulo.pt/mobile **M**

Responsive

Next, I want to highlight responsive design as a technique for adapting to mobile users. Before diving in, let's clear up some terminology. In the early days of responsive design we actually had two separate approaches: One was called Responsive Design, the other Adaptive Design. Early on, responsive design was thought of as fully fluid layouts that flex to fit the available space. In contrast, adaptive layouts were those that use multiple fixed-width designs in order to optimize the interface for various device sizes.

At this point, most of the industry refers to both of these as responsive and the term adaptive seems to be falling out of usage. At times adaptive and responsive are interchangeable. So for this book I have considered a responsive site to be based on a fluid design, a series of fixed width layouts or some combination of both. You will note as well that the next chapter of this book is based entirely on fluid designs (skip to that chapter for details on why I have done this).

Okay, enough with the semantics of all this: Let's take a look at some inspiring examples.

I love the United Pixelworkers website for so many reasons, and I especially love their approach to responsive design **(FIGURES 1, 2 AND 3)**. This modular design lends itself naturally to being responsive. The block-based elements don't interconnect in any way, making them easy to mash around and style for any screen size. This sort of approach is popular in the world of responsive design, if only for the practicalities associated with it.

Another wonderful example that also exhibits a very common approach is The Skool **(FIGURES 4, 5 AND 6)**. This site is built on a series of horizontal bands. Each of these remains in order as the screen size changes, though each band of content adapts. This approach allows the designer and developer to address issues with each block of content individually.

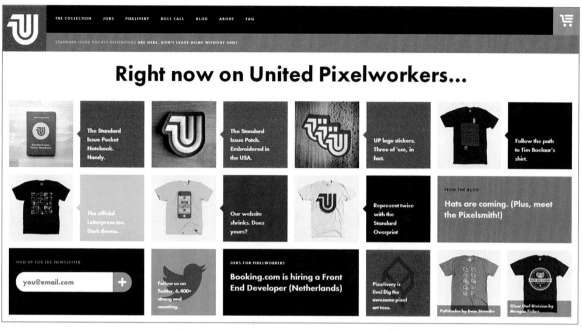

FIGURES 1, 2 AND 3: www.unitedpixelworkers.com 🅓

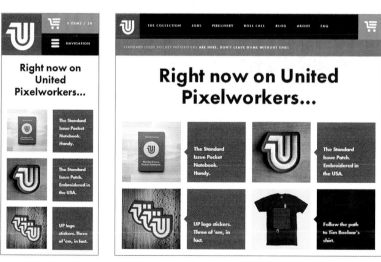

Ⓜ   Ⓣ

FIGURES 4, 5, AND 6: http://theskoolrocks.com Ⓓ

Ⓣ

Ⓜ

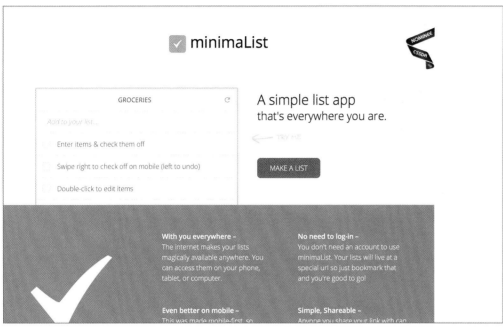

http://getminimalist.com ▶

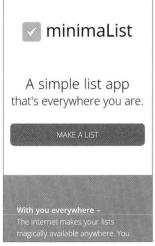

Ⓜ

Ⓣ

espiratecnologias.com **D**

T

M

www.farfromclose.com

M

T

http://kwhome.net

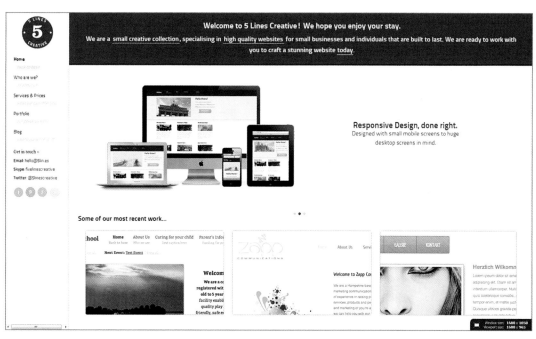

www.5lin.es Ⓓ

Ⓜ

Ⓣ

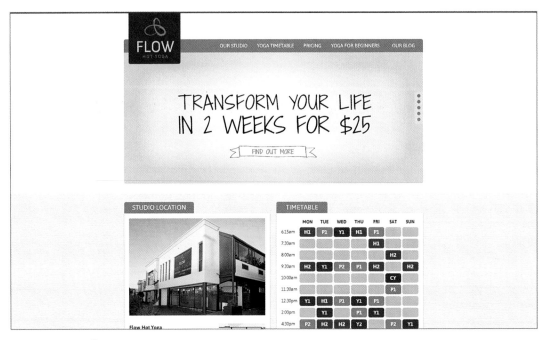

www.flowhotyoga.co.nz

Fluid

Finally, I want to look at some sites entirely based on a fluid approach. As I mentioned earlier, fluid sites are a subset of responsive design. I have chosen to highlight this subset here, as designing a fluid site is a rather difficult task. The following sites do a particularly good job of dealing with some common issues.

One of my favorite examples is the personal site of Javier Lo **(FIGURE 1)**. This site has almost no structural design elements. There are some horizontal lines separating elements, but for the most part, it is simply a typographic site. As such, it is well suited to a fluid approach. You will no doubt notice that the design doesn't just scale to fit the space, it also adapts along the way. Load these sites up in a web browser and then resize the browser to see this in action. For example, note how the layout of the header region with the logo and navigation changes once the size gets to a specific breakpoint. It snaps to a center-aligned approach. Finally, you will perhaps notice that the layout has a maximum width. Just because a design is fluid doesn't mean it has to size up infinitely. If this site could do so, it would grow to widths that would make the content painful to read. By maxing out the width at some point, the designer is able to ensure the content is easy to read.

You will also find this maximum width approach at work on the Usman Group site **(FIGURE 2)**. While the design maxes out, I love that they have the scrolling bar of banners fill the entire space. This large visual element works well beyond the limited width of the rest of the content. By merging the two approaches, they have produced a really slick site. It is amazing to me how powerful simple ideas can be.

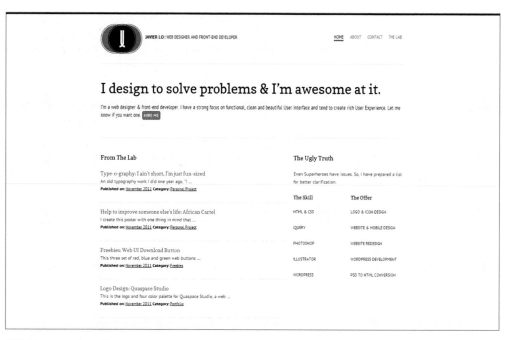

FIGURE 1: www.javierlo.com

FIGURE 2: www.usmangroup.com **D**

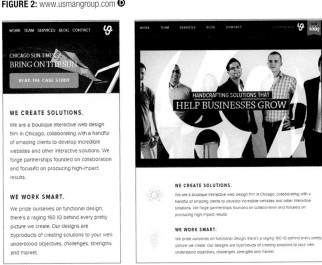

M

T

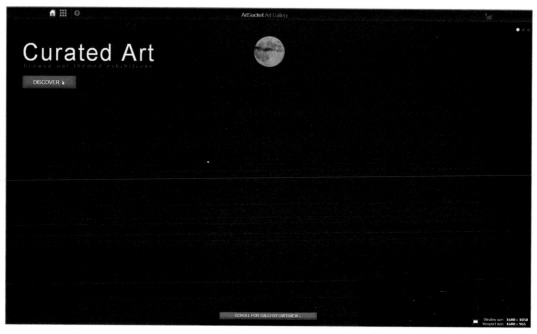

www.artsocket.com Ⓓ

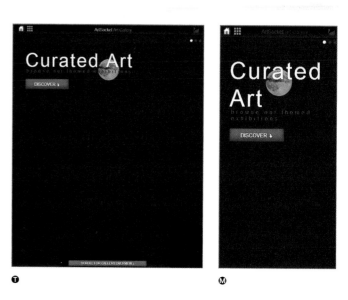

Ⓣ

Ⓜ

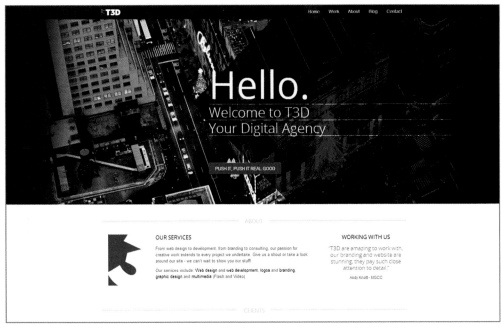

www.t3dhq.com Ⓓ

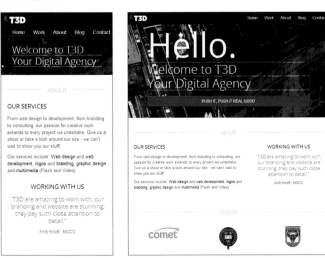

Ⓜ   Ⓣ

03

Frameworks

In the world of mobile design and development, one of the most powerful changes has been the development of a variety of frameworks. A framework is nothing more than a prepackaged set of code that gives our work a boost by dealing with the most common needs. Perhaps the most popular framework is jQuery. jQuery is a collection of functions written in JavaScript, so a front-end developer can do common tasks without having to reinvent the basic elements every time.

For several years we had some minor progress in the world of frameworks, as it pertained to the mobile web. However, with the explosion of responsive design, the complexities of addressing mobile needs greatly increased. As a result, frameworks that dealt with these complexities became more valuable, so an explosion of work has occurred in this area.

In this section I will cover two fundamental types of frameworks. The first are development frameworks: They provide HTML, CSS and JavaScript code that addresses how the website or application will look and function. Second, we will look at what are typically called CSS frameworks. These are typically focused on how a site will lay out and adapt—for example, dealing with how the column structure of a page will adapt at various screen sizes.

A prime example of a development framework is jQuery Mobile (an extension of the core jQuery library specifically made for mobile websites). This framework not only provides a certain visual style, but also deals with the flow of pages and so much more. In contrast, a tool like Bootstrap is really focused on the visual structure, in particular, the column structures. And of course this is all complicated by the fact that many tools blur the lines. The Bootstrap framework, for example, has extensions you can add on that deal with many elements that border on core development issues.

As a designer looking for visual inspiration, my intention is not to endorse or explain any specific framework. Rather, if you happen to be using one, I want to highlight what is possible. And if neither of these apply, this section can be yet another series of gorgeous sites that you can pluck your favorite ideas from.

jQuery Mobile

I am a huge fan of jQuery, and I am equally enthusiastic about jQuery Mobile. This awesome framework is built on top of jQuery and the jQuery UI. It is relatively easy to skin (that is, to apply a custom design to the interface) and is backed by the same folks as the core jQuery library. Its stability, ease of use and smooth functionality makes it a popular choice for many.

Often, you will find that many of the default styles and approaches built into the jQuery library make their way into most sites built on it. Not surprisingly, the most common problem designers have with a framework like this is that all the sites built on it tend to look the same. This is, of course, why I have tried as much as possible to include a diverse set of sites that push the boundaries of what the framework provides. In fact, I think you will be pleased to see that none of the samples provided here feel "default" in any way. They each feel very distinct and have been clearly pushed far beyond the framework's default styles. This makes them even better sources of inspiration!

One of my favorite approaches on the mobile web is a super-clean, portal-style approach. We find exactly that on the Enizyme website **(FIGURE 1)**. Here, the prominent logo clearly establishes the brand's name on the site. Three simple navigation elements—complete with icons and text—help you dive into the site. Note that the navigation is spelled out; you don't just get icons to click on in hopes of finding what you want.

Boozt.com also takes on a portal-style home page, but with a lot more options **(FIGURE 2)**. Clearly, this e-commerce site has much deeper content than the previous sample, and yet the home page takes on very much the same approach. Clear, easy to understand—and more importantly—easy to *touch* buttons on the home page help visitors dig into the section they want most.

Next, I want to take a quick look at the Visit Idaho mobile site **(FIGURE 3)**. The large image is important in establishing the mood of the site. The fact that the large image takes up most of your initial screen is something I would likely question. However, in this case, the approach is spot on and clearly informs the visitor of the site's purpose. Another detail I appreciate about this site is the navigation: The large buttons are easy to click and have short text on them to explain what lies below. I really appreciate that they have a simple list below the main text detailing what you will find in each link. This extra bit of information helps me easily find the content I am looking for.

Finally, I want to point out that the sites showcased here based on jQuery Mobile are all mobile-specific sites. That is to say, they are designed to be used on a phone. While jQuery Mobile works on desktops, its real mission is addressing the needs of phone-based users, and it is really ideally suited for mobile devices. This makes it a popular choice among those building mobile-specific sites.

MORE ON JQUERY MOBILE: http://jquerymobile.com.

FIGURE 1: www.enizyme.com/m

FIGURE 2: m.boozt.com/eu/en

FIGURE 3: www.visitidaho.org/m

www.dls.com.py/mobile

m.century21.be

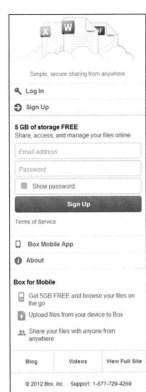

m.box.com

m.toptable.co.uk

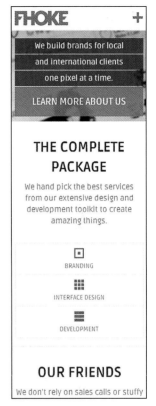

www.fhoke.com

http://arunpattnaik.com

m.cheapoair.com

IKEA m.ikea.com

http://ssidebgclub.com

m.toogethr.com Ⓜ

www.bookrenter.com/m Ⓜ

http://beantowndesign.com/themes/
mobilize/demos/1/index.html Ⓜ

http://beantowndesign.com/themes/
emdot/5/index.html Ⓜ

Bootstrap

Bootstrap (formerly known as Twitter Bootstrap) is a CSS framework for building responsive websites. Its core is a 12-column grid system for building sites, and one of the primary options you will likely want to include is a responsive extension that adapts the 12 columns to fit a wide range of screen sizes.

I want to highlight that these samples look nothing like each other—and nothing like the default styles included with Bootstrap. Yes, the styles Bootstrap comes with are slick and nice. And in a pinch they can be helpful if you're just throwing something simple together. But if you want to do more, you want a system that is easy to extend. Fortunately, as you can see here, Bootstrap clearly allows you to take total control of your design. It really is more about providing a structural framework than anything else.

One simple detail that I think is important to consider as you design a responsive site is the number of columns you create. For example, the MacGuru Consulting website **(FIGURE 1)** has three blocks of content under the home page banner area. This trio looks great on the desktop and phone sizes, but notice how the three struggle to fill the space on the tablet version. When you have three columns, the only options are to shrink the columns or to stack them up—there is no intermediate step. Contrast this with DennisErny.com **(FIGURE 2),** where you see four items in the recent projects list. These four nicely stack into a 2×2 grid or in a single column and, of course, four across, side by side. By simply using an even number of items, the designer has more options. Clearly, at times we must use an odd number of columns, but it is a powerful trick to keep in mind, as it has a significant impact on your options.

MORE ON BOOTSTRAP: http://twitter.github.com/bootstrap

FIGURE 1: http://macguruconsulting.com ⓣ   ⓜ

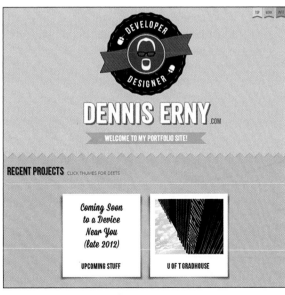

FIGURE 2: http://denniserny.com ⓣ   ⓜ

http://thebagelbars.com ⊤

Ⓜ

www.gusta.com Ⓜ

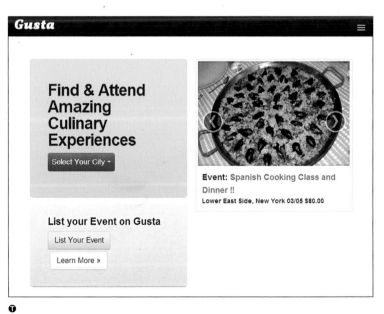

⊤

http://hiddendepth.ie ●T

●M

www.reputationradar.it ●T

●M

HTML5 Boilerplate

Like many frameworks, HTML5 Boilerplate includes the essential components for structuring web pages. But where Boilerplate excels is in the area of extras. Instead of custom building all of their own solutions to various problems, they simply make use of the best options in the industry. Additionally, the framework is geared toward giving you a solid foundation to build on, not necessarily toward giving you an initial style set. This is a strong differentiation from Bootstrap (page 32), which is largely based on a default set of styles. The reality is that Boilerplate tends to be more developer-friendly.

Given that this is more of a technical foundation and less a visual one, it should come as no surprise that the sites presented here bear no resemblance to each other, or to some default styles associated with the framework. In fact, the point of this framework is that it enables designers and developers to create sites based on entirely unique designs.

A nice demonstration of this open-ended set of possibilities is the contrast between The Brooklyn Brewery Mash site **(FIGURE 1)** and the Gateway Bank site **(FIGURE 2)** These sites have entirely different structures, totally different styles and are completely tailored to the needs of the given project. It can be really tempting to mash sites into specific structures in order to save time and money. But here we see that with a looser structure and style, we end up with more tailored sites. I believe this is one reason developers in particular love this tool. It gets them going without locking them into anything in terms of the final site structure.

You will also no doubt notice that the sites built on Boilerplate—at least those shown here—are responsive. In fact, the framework provides a lot of structure that makes it very easy to get started with responsive design. I highly recommend this framework if you want to code from scratch, but get a tremendous jump start.

MORE ON HTML5 BOILERPLATE: http://html5boilerplate.com

FIGURE 1: http://brooklynbrewerymash.com ⦿

FIGURE 2: http://gcbaz.com Ⓜ   ⦿

Join Our Team

We are on the hunt for some passionate, talented and highly-motivated individuals to craft and develop beautiful, enjoyable and usable interactive experiences.

www.creativesoapbox.com Ⓜ

Ⓣ

http://friesengallery.com Ⓣ

Ⓜ

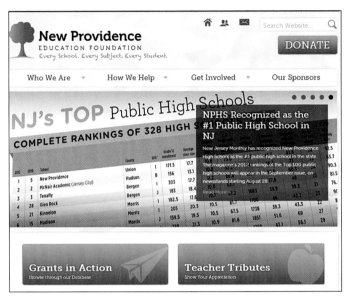

http://npedfoundation.org 🅣

Ⓜ

www.copio.us 🅣

Ⓜ

960 Grid System

The 960 Grid System is largely based on the particular screen size. This framework was originally designed to fit perfectly on screens 1024 pixels wide. The 960 Grid provides a set of column structures to build around, making it super easy to code sites designed on top of this grid. Fortunately, the system has been extended and updated to accommodate responsive sites. The 960 Grid is one of the older—and most widely used—frameworks. And though other frameworks are beginning to displace it, it continues to be a viable option.

One thing about this framework that is super easy to love is the assets provided. You can download template files for Photoshop, Fireworks and much more. Included in these are guides for the underlying grid structure. This makes it quick and easy to start designing with the framework in mind. And at the end of the day, a grid system is a powerful design tool in any medium, so it is a natural fit and a common theme in many of the frameworks listed here.

In some samples the grid system shines through rather vividly. For example, on the site of Jann de Vries **(FIGURE 1),** we can easily see the column structure as it renders on a tablet device. In contrast, you will see that the site collapses to what appears to be a single column in the phone version of the site.

Another example where this column structure is vividly seen is the Boyle Heights site **(FIGURE 2)**. Compare the tablet version to the phone version. This illustrates rather clearly how using a common-sized column system across your site makes it far easier to collapse down to a mobile version.

In other cases, the grid system doesn't show itself as clearly. Take the Big Bite Creative site, for example **(FIGURE 3)**. Here the grid is invisible. And as you no doubt realize by now, flexibility is a critical factor in picking a solid framework on which to build a website.

MORE ON 960 GRID SYSTEM VISIT: http://960.gs

FIGURE 1: www.min-style.de ● ⓜ

FIGURE 2: www.bhlc.net ●

ⓜ

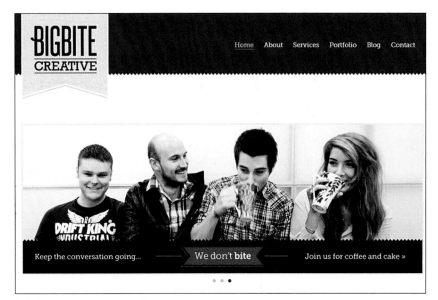

FIGURE 3: http://bigbitecreative.com ⓣ ⓜ

ⓜ www.gantry-framework.org ⓣ

www.mooscandybar.co.uk 🅣

 🅜

http://interactionhero.com 🅣

320 and Up

Of all the frameworks presented here, 320 and Up is rather unique. In fact, of all the frameworks I am aware of, this is the only of its type. 320 and Up takes a mobile-first approach. It is geared toward providing a mobile-friendly interface first and foremost. Instead of collapsing down, it is intended to expand out as the screen size increases. This framework hinges its philosophy and approach on the fact that mobile web traffic is rapidly increasing and is in fact predicted to overtake desktop computer use sometime in 2014. This turning point highlights the need to cater to mobile users, and the 320 and Up system takes this to heart.

While this framework isn't as wildly popular as many of the others here, I have included it, as I believe it is a preview of the web ten years from now. With the current explosion of mobile and tablet devices, it isn't hard to imagine them becoming the majority of web traffic.

Frankly speaking, many people find it hard to imagine a mobile-first design; it just feels like a rather radical step. Fortunately, we have a few examples to look at. First, I want to consider the personal blog of Steve Fisher **(FIGURE 1)**. This site looks and feels similar to many of the mobile sites showcased in this book. I would argue, however, that it has one rather big distinction. Many responsive sites feel so mashed together, but Steve's site feels extremely streamlined and its mobile-first approach shines through. Interestingly, as you see it scale up, it works remarkably well and is entirely free of visual clutter. It turns out that a mobile-first mentality actually helps you focus more vividly on your site's core purposes. Instead of lots of extra "stuff," Steve has packed his site with meaty content to sink your teeth into. We could all learn a lot from this approach, and I believe it will only become more prominent in time.

MORE ON 320 AND UP: http://stuffandnonsense.co.uk/projects/320andup

FIGURE 1: http://hellofisher.com Ⓜ Ⓣ

Ⓓ

http://fifasoccerblog.com

D

http://zookeeper.com **M**

T

D

Foundation

Foundation is a site-building framework built by Zurb, a design company that specializes in building incredible websites. They also invest heavily in a large range of tools and products for the web community. Foundation is one of these tools. This framework is the by-product of an agency that does client work and puts out lots of free tools. As such it has its roots in the business world (ensuring it has a dose of reality built into it), Foundation has found a large following.

While Foundation has many of the basic elements we would expect—like a grid system and responsive design features built right in—it does have one nice twist. It includes a number of resources that enable you to very rapidly prototype websites. While many designers still prefer to design in Photoshop first, there is a growing movement toward design and prototyping in the browser. This tool rather vividly supports this and leverages it as a key selling point.

One of my favorite examples in this chapter is the Styli.se website **(FIGURE 1)**. There are several reasons for this. First, in terms of mobile sites, this example fits into a rather small category, visually speaking. The trend for mobile sites leans heavily toward minimalism, and this site, with its visual decoration, sets it apart. This actually presents a huge opportunity for mobile designers in terms of a way to stand out. No, I don't suggest overdoing it, but there is definitely the potential to stand out in the space just by being more decorative. (If you want more on this idea, check out the Decorative chapter in this book on page 108.) Another key to this site is that it maintains a strong sense of hierarchy as it collapses down, a trait that is sometimes lost as a site shrinks for smaller screens. In this case, you can easily digest the content and quickly scan it based on the hierarchy of the content.

MORE ON FOUNDATION: http://foundation.zurb.com.

FIGURE 1: http://styli.se

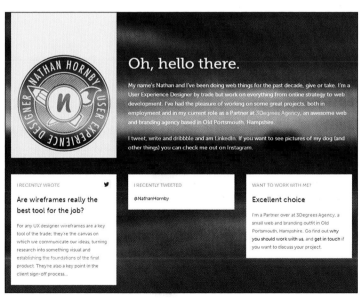

www.nathanhornby.com

HOME ABOUT PORTFOLIO BLOG CONTACT

3Degrees is a small web design agency that creates beautiful user experiences for all devices.

WHY WORK WITH US?

RECENT WORK
Cogenta Branding, web design & development.

3 REASONS YOU'LL LOVE WORKING WITH US

WE'RE DIFFERENT
We think you'll love working with us, here's 3 great reasons why!

OUR PROCESS
Find out who we are, where we work and how our process can help you.

www.3degreesagency.com Ⓣ

HOME ABOUT PORTFOLIO BLOG CONTACT

3Degrees is a small web design agency that creates beautiful user experiences for all devices.

WHY WORK WITH US?

RECENT WORK
Cogenta Branding, web design & development.

3 REASONS YOU'LL LOVE WORKING WITH US

Ⓜ

Jacqueline West, Writer

Home
About
Events/Schools
Journal
Books
Other Writing

THE BOOKS OF ELSEWHERE
Volume Three:
The Second Spy

New York Times best seller The Books of Elsewhere, Jacqueline West's award-winning fantasy series for young readers, is published by Dial in the USA and will also be published in Italy, Spain, Greece, Turkey, Indonesia,

Ⓜ

www.jacquelinewest.com Ⓣ

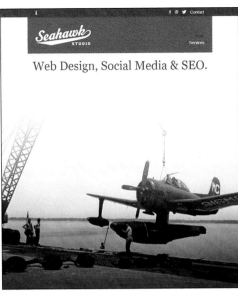

http://seahawkstudio.com ⊕

Ⓜ

Ⓜ

www.letstravelsomewhere.com ⊕

Less Framework

Each framework tends to have a core focus, and with Less Framework, it is all about adaptive design. If you remember, adaptive design is simply a specific version of responsive design. (For more details on this, see the Responsive chapter on page 10.) Less Framework is a CSS-based grid system that collapses down as the size of the screen decreases. It is based on four different layouts, each leveraging distinct typography presets and grids.

One of the real perks of this system is the community of resources that have been built around it. Often, it is through these extended resources that you truly find the efficiency of a framework.

Strangely, the examples I ended up collecting for this chapter actually share a fairly common visual style. They are all very type-centered and are based on solid colors, in large part. This has little to nothing to do with the framework. It is much more about the fact that this is simply a currently popular style (see Flat Pixels on page 105). Much like the other frameworks featured here, this system is more about giving you a solid structure, and less about locking you into a visual style.

One example I would like to highlight is the personal site of Naomi Atkinson **(FIGURE 1)**. What I appreciate about this example is that it contains a large amount of content. With responsive design, a site can be much easier to implement if your content is in short quantity. In contrast, this content-rich site demonstrates that it is entirely possible to adapt dense sites to mobile screens. Sure it takes more work, but as you can see here, the results can be well worth it. In this case, a solid framework that supports a collapsing design is a critical component.

MORE ON LESS FRAMEWORK VISIT: http://lessframework.com.

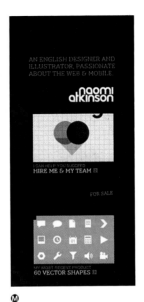

FIGURE 1: http://naomiatkinson.com

Shoperize

Discover a brand new M-Commerce experience with Shoperize. Fast, ergonomic, simple & efficient, you can now have your eCommerce business accessible on mobile phones & tablets in order to increase your sales and conversion rate.

Shoperize is compatible with all major eCommerce platforms

www.shoperize.com

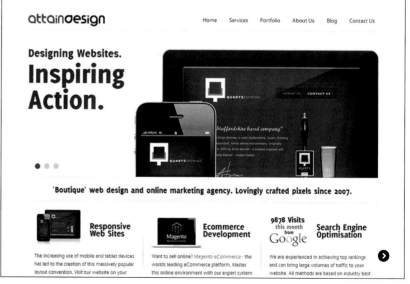

www.attaindesign.co.uk

www.madebysplendid.com ⊤

Ⓜ

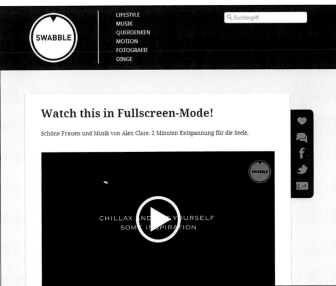

http://swabble.me ⊤

Ⓜ

04

Responsive Elements

As a natural part of surveying the responsive work of others one finds themselves constantly resizing their web browser. It can be hard enough to hunt around the web for design samples fitting your needs. And with responsive design this time-consuming task is exponentially more difficult as you have to surf around constantly resizing your browser. With this in mind, I have built this section to feature key elements and—more importantly, to show a diverse range of solutions to a single problem. In this way, we can get a nice range of ideas around a single topic, hopefully fulfilling the idea generation goals of this book.

Navigation

I could probably write an entire book that dissects, showcases and reviews various approaches to navigation and how it can adapt in a responsive environment. Given the limited space I have here, I had to work hard to find a range of solutions. Also, I hate to just talk about the same popular sites everyone else does, so I had to be sure to include some fresh meat. Personally, I am excited at the results. Let's dive in.

First, I want to highlight the Symphony Online site **(FIGURE 1)**. In the two screenshots of this site, you will notice that the main navigation changes from a list of plain text elements on the desktop version to a stacked list of buttons on the mobile layout. This shift is critical because it caters to the primary interface tool on each. The desktop version works great for those using a mouse and is just what you would expect. In contrast, the mobile version relies on the user touching it with their finger. In this situation, a much larger visual target is perfect for the job. Not only does it give you a larger target but it also has another key benefit. When you touch something on your screen, you can no longer see the element. So if the text is changing color to indicate that you touched it—you can't see it. In contrast, these large buttons provide a large enough visual element that the user can easily see what has happened based on the part of the button that extends well beyond their finger. This adds a great deal of comfort and removes the stress of trying to touch the right thing. This simple approach keeps the user in mind and is a critical tool in the designer's toolbox.

Another key problem you might face with navigation is space. Take the New Zealand Beauty Expo site, for example **(FIGURE 2)**. This site contains a rather large list of links in the primary navigation. On a horizontal navigation bar, it is a lot to take in. In the mobile version, you will notice that the items are stacked. More importantly—they are all hidden away in the little box with three lines. My screenshot here shows the menu in its expanded state. This method hides the navigation away until needed and keeps it from being a hindrance to the site. This little widget is often referred to as a "navicon"—short for a navigation icon.

There are many other nuances and lessons to be learned from the navigation samples here. You will also find a great deal of inspiration in many of the other chapters that happen to show various approaches to navigation as a site responds to its environment. Given the crucial nature of navigation, I encourage you to explore many different options in this area.

FIGURE 1: www.symphonyonline.co.uk

FIGURE 2: www.nzbeautyexpo.com

1020concepts

about   clients   contact   directions   Call us: +31 (0)6 484 282 56

TenTwentyConcepts, webdesign & development, user experience & optimalisation. We build your website for mobile & desktop, you enjoy the ride!

WHY 1020CONCEPTS

1020concepts is owned by Evert Slagter, (web)designer & developer, with over 10 years of experience building websites.

The Ten – Twenty in 1020concepts stands for the time we work in a day, from ten (10:00) in the morning till eight (20:00) in the evening. (But 1020concepts should be called, 10 – 24 or maybe 24 – 7 concepts)

1020concepts is not a standard full service internet agency. 1020concepts works together with the right kind of people who are specialized in their field, to give our clients the best solution possible.See our partners.

THE WORK

1020concepts designs and builds elegant, easy to use, websites with the latest techniques like HTML5, CSS3 and Javascript. We make websites that work on different platform by using "responsive" techniques and a "mobile first" approche. We use our own Content Management System (1020cms) or systems like Drupal and Wordpress. All our websites are hand-coded from start till finish.

If you are interested in a new website or a complete makeover of your current website. Please, don't hesitate to call us + 31 6 484 282 56.

http://1020concepts.nl ❶

1020concepts

TenTwentyConcepts, webdesign & development, user experience & optimalisation. We build your website for mobile & desktop, you enjoy the ride!

Ⓜ

TGD   ABOUT   ARCHIVE

BOBBY SOLOMON

ABOUT BOBBY

Bobby Solomon is the founder and editor-in-chief of The Fox Is Black, a blog that focuses on design, music, and culture in general. He currently lives in Los Angeles where he works as an art director at Disney Interactive. He has a boyfriend named Kyle, who runs TFIB sister site, Los Angeles, I'm Yours, and together they have the two most awesome dogs on earth—Dottie and Scooter.

· thefoxisblack.com · @thefoxisblack · Facebook

http://thegreatdiscontent.com ❶

TGD   ABOUT   ARCHIVE

BOBBY SOLOMON

ABOUT BOBBY

Bobby Solomon is the founder and editor-in-chief of The Fox Is Black, a blog that focuses on design, music, and culture in general. He currently lives in Los Angeles where he works as an art director at Disney Interactive. He has a boyfriend named Kyle, who runs TFIB sister site, Los Angeles, I'm Yours, and together they have the two most awesome dogs on earth—Dottie and Scooter.

· thefoxisblack.com · @thefoxisblack · Facebook

Ⓜ

http://fringewebdevelopment.com ⓣ

ⓜ

ⓜ

http://syncconf.com ⓣ

Logos

When it comes to responsive design, it can be overwhelming to deal with every last nuance of a website. As such, it can be easy to forget elements that we might like to custom handle. I think logos are a prime example of this. I know my instinct is to say that a logo should remain the same no matter what; the consistency just seems important. The following collection of sites has changed my mind on this matter. In fact, I now think that the logo is one of the *most* important elements we can consider modifying as screen sizes change.

A prime example of this is App Cube **(FIGURE 1)**. In this example the logo undergoes a rather significant change, depending on the device size. On the desktop it is left aligned and the visual is richer. The text is also larger. On the small screen you will note that it is set up to be center aligned, have smaller text and a single color. The logo is custom tailored to each environment.

Another example that takes this approach is the Sycamore School website **(FIGURE 2)**. Here, the logo undergoes rather minor tweaks and shifts from a taller two-line format to a single line. This helps to greatly minimize the header bar and allows the content to appear much higher on the page. Consider how large the header would have to be if the logo were the same. Subtle shifts like this are powerful to help ensure each site operates at its best.

On the Hicksdesign website we see another example of subtle changes that have a significant impact on the final product **(FIGURE 3)**. In this case, the logo has a decorative attachment that moves from being left-aligned to being centered. It's a small change that has no impact on the branding of the site, but does affect the balance and overall feel of the site.

Not every brand is going to be open to changes like this. I am sure if you tell Coca-Cola that they need to change their logo to fit your design, you will get a less than positive response. However, there are countless situations where tweaking the logo a bit will yield great results.

FIGURE 1: http://appcube.info ☍

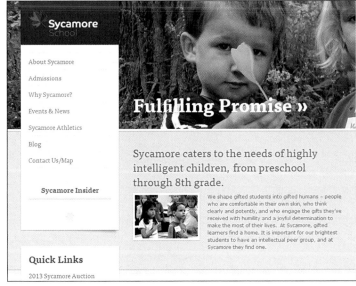

FIGURE 2: http://sycamoreschool.org ☍

FIGURE 3: http://hicksdesign.co.uk ❶   Ⓜ

Ⓜ

www.deren.me ❶

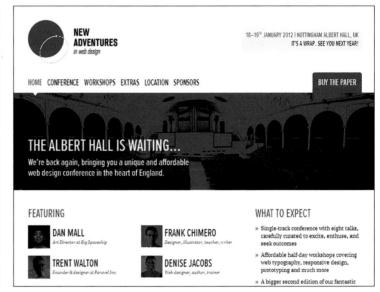

http://2012.newadventuresconf.com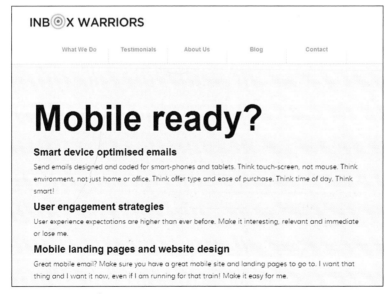

www.inboxwarriors.co.uk

Calls to Action

A call to action is the primary goal of your website. When a visitor lands on your site, there is some goal you'd like them to accomplish. It might be to make a purchase, register for an event, join your newsletter or simply call you. The point is that your site is there to serve a purpose and push potential clients towards a target. These call-to-action elements are the buttons that take people toward that goal. In this chapter I not only want to look at some call-to-action buttons, but also at how they have been worked into a responsive site.

A nice example to start with is the United Utilities website **(FIGURE 1)**. This site is packed with a lot of content and the home page is packed with links: In fact, it is pretty much a giant link portal. Through all of this, the site appears to have three key calls to action. You will see them in the large green buttons. Note that these buttons manage to break through the clutter to some degree and stand out. Now, take a look at how this site adapted to mobile. That huge array of links becomes a series of lists. If you look at the desktop version, there are theoretically many things that could have come before the three call-to-action buttons. However, you will see that they are given top placement in the mobile version and this ensures that they show up on the first view of the site. In general, as you translate a site to mobile, you really have to keep your mission in mind—as this site has done.

Another nice example of this is the Atlanta Ballet **(FIGURE 2)**. Here, the orange button beckons for users to buy tickets. They make sure that no matter the screen size, the button is visible when the page initially loads. This ensures that users can always see where to buy tickets. Though the site might have many content elements that help you know what the company is up to, what they really want is for you to buy tickets. Keeping this core mission in mind clearly impacted the way they adapted the call to action across devices.

Finally, take a look at the Fresh Tilled Soil site **(FIGURE 3)**. On this desktop site, you will not notice a call to action. It is clearly a portfolio site, but the steps they want you to take are not apparent. Contrast this with the mobile version and you will notice something interesting. Here, two clear action items are prominently placed: They are colored in a highly visible way and direct users towards key steps. Understanding the context and the different needs of each situation is something that sometimes gets lost in responsive design. Here, we see that an experience can easily be catered to the environment of the user.

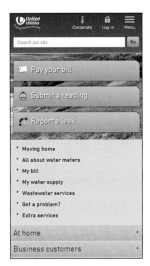
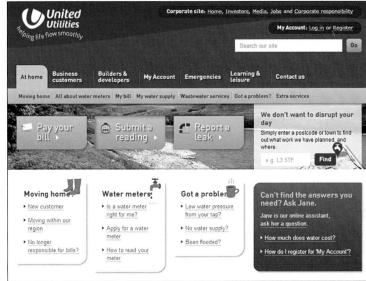

M

FIGURE 1: www.unitedutilities.com

FIGURE 2: www.atlantaballet.com

FIGURE 3: www.freshtilledsoil.com ⓣ

http://fringewebdevelopment.com/orbit-wordpress-development-framework ⓣ

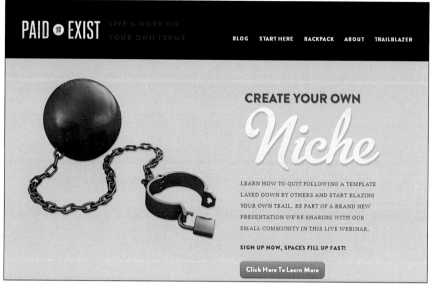

 http://paidtoexist.com ⊕

http://silvertonhealth.org ⊕

Promo Space

An incredibly common part of many home pages is a prominent promo space. In this critical space, designers often communicate the core purpose of the website. Typically we find a large to-the-point sales pitch that sums up the service. This is often matched with a smaller but more in-depth description of the product or service. Next, we usually find a screenshot or image of the product. Finally, many of these promo spaces finish off with a call to action, compelling the user to take some critical step. The end result is a powerful marketing space that attempts to quickly connect with visitors and spur them on to becoming customers.

A perfect demonstration of these elements is the Salesforce Desk website **(FIGURE 1)**. In this example we find all of these components. And as you can see in the screenshots here, these elements adapt nicely to fit a variety of screens, including tablets and smartphones. As with many responsive designs, the contents tend to end up stacked on top of each other. In this case, I really appreciate the focus on the call-to-action buttons that remain near the top of the screen. Depending on your layout it might be tempting to push them down, but I encourage you to consider keeping them high up and on the first screen visitors see.

The Advanced Custom Fields website is another nice demonstration of adapting promo space to various screen sizes **(FIGURE 2)**. In this case, the call to action actually increases in size and importance as the screen size decreases. Though for this particular content, I would argue that this is not the most critical element on a small screen: After all, I doubt many people will download this WordPress plugin to their smartphones! Technicalities aside, the site vividly demonstrates how this promo space can nicely scale.

Finally, I want to highlight the promo space on the Yacket site **(FIGURE 3)**. The promo space adapts as you might predict; however, on the smallest of screens the images disappear. Don't be afraid to take radical steps toward condensing your site for smaller devices. It can be scary, but as in this case, the results speak volumes. The promo space takes up a much more reasonable amount of space on smaller devices and continues to communicate the site's purpose.

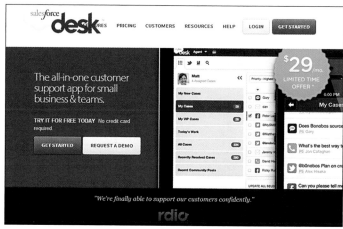

FIGURE 1: www.desk.com Ⓣ

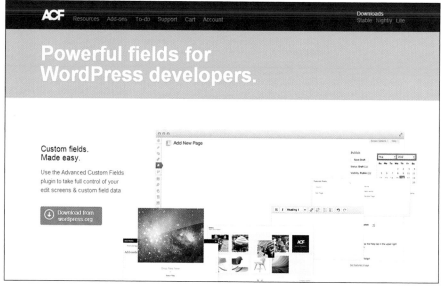

FIGURE 2: www.advancedcustomfields.com Ⓣ

FIGURE 3: http://yacket.com ●

Ⓜ

http://pro.buysellads.com ●

M

www.cutandslice.me **T**

http://fineuploader.com **T**

M

Sliders

When it comes to popular web widgets, none seems to have attained the popularity that the standard image slider has. One can hardly visit a site without finding one on a home page. There is a huge range of pre-built options to choose from and it is so easy to pack lots of content into one. In my opinion, it seems that they have become a dumping ground for all the "stuff" clients want to pack into a home page. As the responsive design movement took hold, sliders took a little longer to catch up. As it turns out, many of these widgets were built on rigid systems that didn't play nice in a changing landscape. Fortunately, many really smart JavaScript masters have tackled the problem, and presented here are a number of examples of responsive sliders in the wild.

One of the most important lessons of the responsive slider is that the structure can (and probably should) change as the screen size changes. It isn't about just scaling it down: Instead, we must reformat the content. Many of the sites here demonstrate this, including the Wentworth Mansion website **(FIGURE 1)**. On larger screens, the content overlays the images. When screen sizes shrink, the slider reformats and places the content below the images. This simple change ensures that the content is easily consumed and tailored to the user's environment. And yes, it does mean you either need to build your own slider or use a slider widget intended to scale nicely in this way.

Another really interesting example is the Modern Green Home site **(FIGURE 2)**. In this case, the slider has a continuous approach. On larger screens, you can see additional slides to each side. As the screen shrinks, the focus shifts to the middle one exclusively. From the beginning, the size of the image is formatted to fit nicely on small screens. Therefore, this site adapts to various screen sizes in a rather unique way.

For another interesting approach look at the Always Creative website **(FIGURE 3)**. In this case, the site uses a slider on mobile screens, but on the desktop/tablet version the content is all displayed in a grid. This less-implemented approach is an interesting solution I believe we could put to work more often.

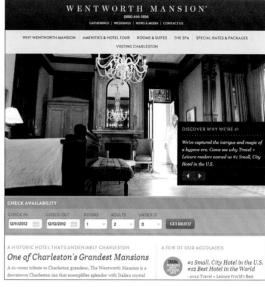

FIGURE 1: www.wentworthmansion.com

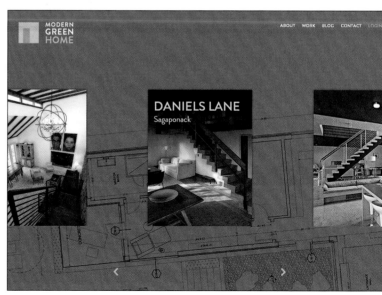

FIGURE 2: http://moderngreenhome.com

FIGURE 3: http://alwayscreative.net ●

Ⓜ

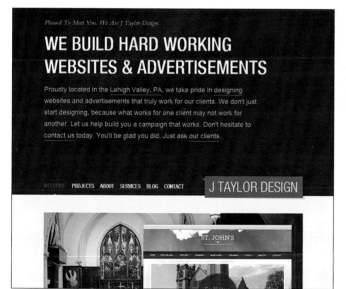

www.thejtsite.com ●

Ⓜ

www.greenbelt.org.uk **T**

http://foodsense.is **T**

http://elementcreative.com ●

●Ⓜ

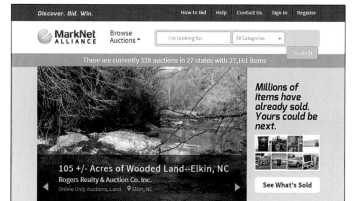

http://marknetalliance.com ●

Ⓜ

Forms

Forms are one of the more complex HTML elements to style and are often the source of much frustration. They are tough to wrangle into place for one layout, and having to style them for multiple layouts makes them even more problematic. Fortunately, one of the best ways to deal with forms is to simply change their layout, not necessarily their styles. Take a look at the samples to see what I mean.

A nice example of this is PurePleasureDesign.com **(FIGURE 1)**. Here, the form controls maintain the exact same look and feel; they simply change in the layout. On the tablet and desktop they are presented as two columns. This structure collapses to a single column on mobile devices.

Another approach that limits the pain of customizing forms for each layout is to focus on the stuff surrounding the form. For example, the form shown from the Burst Creative site stays pretty much the same regardless of the device size **(FIGURE 2)**. You will see in the images that the sidebar is moved as the page shrinks and the form controls simply scale down in their width. This ensures that the forms fit on the screen without much effort. We find a similar approach on the samples from Aleks Faure's site. **(FIGURE 3)**.

In order to limit the pain, we can also plan a design that easily shrinks. You can find this approach on the Learndot website **(FIGURE 4)**. Here, the form is set up in a single column. As the screen shrinks, elements around the form disappear and the form fields simply shrink horizontally. This simplistic approach is relatively easy to accommodate and minimizes the extra work of restyling the form for each screen size.

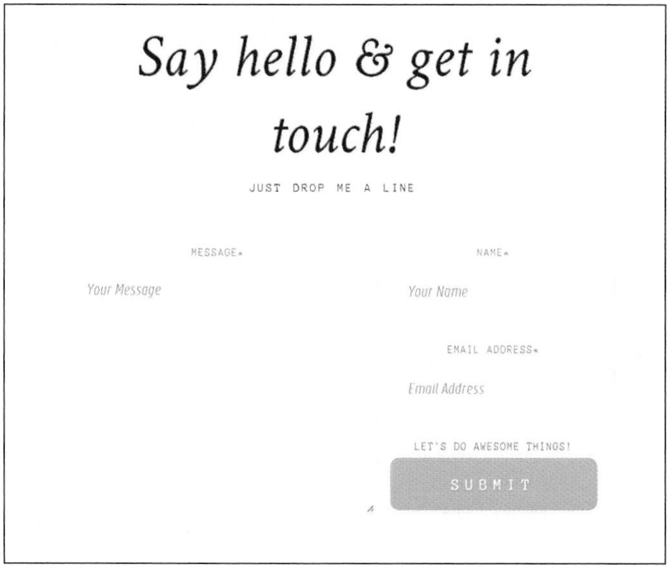

Say hello & get in touch!

JUST DROP ME A LINE

MESSAGE*

Your Message

NAME*

Your Name

EMAIL ADDRESS*

Email Address

LET'S DO AWESOME THINGS!

SUBMIT

MESSAGE*

Your Message

NAME*

Your Name

EMAIL ADDRESS*

Email Address

LET'S DO AWESOME THINGS!

SUBMIT

FIGURE 1: www.purepleasuredesign.com/en/kontakt ⊤ Ⓜ

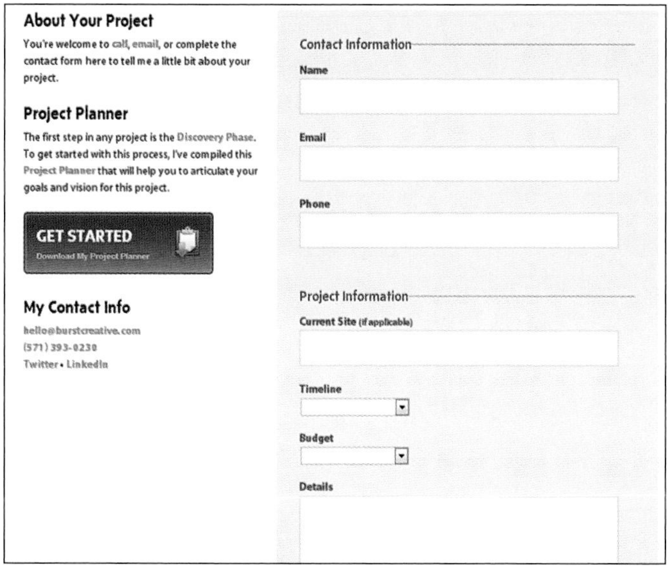

About Your Project

You're welcome to call, email, or complete the contact form here to tell me a little bit about your project.

Project Planner

The first step in any project is the Discovery Phase. To get started with this process, I've compiled this Project Planner that will help you to articulate your goals and vision for this project.

GET STARTED
Download My Project Planner

My Contact Info

hello@burstcreative.com
(571) 393-0230
Twitter • LinkedIn

Contact Information

Name

Email

Phone

Project Information

Current Site (if applicable)

Timeline

Budget

Details

Contact Information

Name

Email

Phone

Project Information

Current Site (if applicable)

Timeline

Budget

Details

FIGURE 2: http://burstcreative.com/contact ⊤ Ⓜ

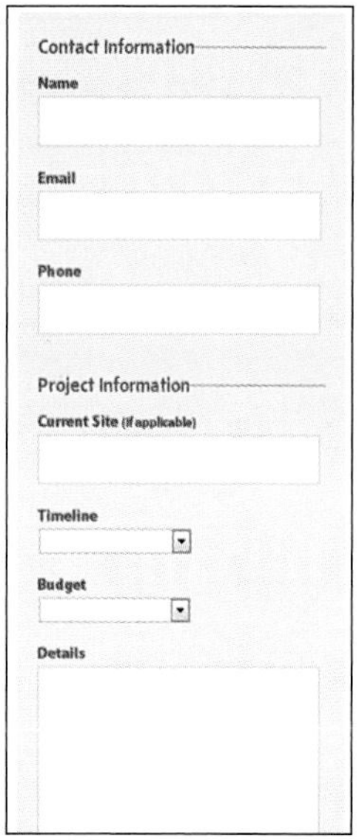

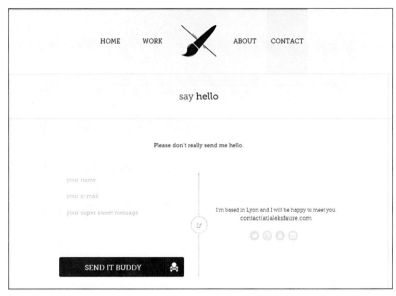

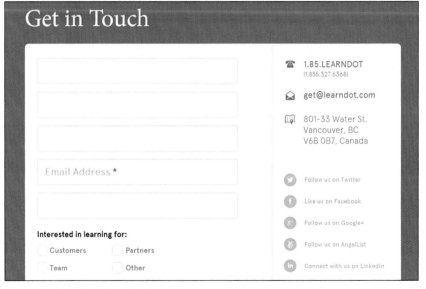

CONTACT

Looking for a project planner? You'll find that on my **other site**.

Enter your name

Your email address

Your message

Send Message

http://henry.brown.name/#contact

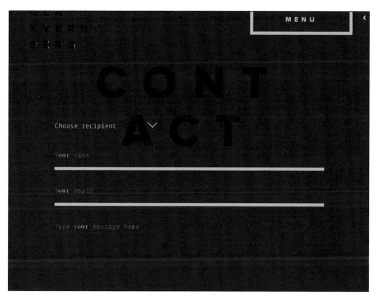

www.olakvernberg.com/contact

Content

With responsive design, it seems that a lot of attention is given to the structure of the site, while the content itself is often left to fend for itself. In many cases this works out okay. But we can actually find many sites that tweak the layout of the content to fit various screen sizes.

In this area, one of the most interesting trends is the introduction of multi-column content. Historically speaking, the web has typically presented content as a large single column. This, however, doesn't necessarily maximize the space available on larger screens. Here you will find several examples that shift from a single column to multiple columns at larger screen sizes.

One of my favorite examples of this is the Introducing the Novel site **(FIGURE 1)**. Notice that on the large screen the content is displayed in three columns, and compressed to a single column on mobile layout. There are a few extra details that I also want to highlight. For example, notice how the layout of the heading changes. Additionally, on the large screen, the first column is left empty except for the icon used for illustration purposes: This supporting element is removed as the screen size shrinks. Yes, it helps communicate the purpose of the site, and the large empty space draws your attention conveniently to the starting point of the content, but it isn't mission critical. So as space is reduced, the element is hidden.

In many cases, content isn't necessarily a stream of words—such as what you might find in a blog or news article. In some cases, the content is a series of products or other items, such as on the Stury site **(FIGURE 2)**. Here, the content is a list of books, including titles, key details and an action button. What I really love about this example is how the formatting changes as the site shifts from desktop to mobile. On the mobile version, the content fits really well in the horizontal bands that you see. It might have been tempting to stick with the vertical approach of each element, as you find on the desktop version, but this would have resulted in a lot of wasted space and potentially very large cover shots. My only complaint is that in all of the layouts the titles are not completely shown. That said, the way this site adapts the content in a responsive way is really solid and a great example to follow.

Introducing
THE NOVEL

A novel is a type of book. Like most new artforms, literary and otherwise, it is a difficult object to define comprehensively, but most typically it can be taken to be a long piece of narrative fiction. Written prose, historically turned towards folk tales, myths, hagiographies and epics, is now being used to tell all sorts of stories about ourselves, the heavens, and everything in between. It may be helpful to think of the novel as a loose genre encompassing all those mentioned above, but also one that allows for stories outside the realm of the fantastical. Stories, to put it simply, about us.

The qualifications (or requirements) of the novel are quite porous. We may say that the novel must contain a single narrative, ruling out collections of short stories, but the novel has been known to break out of this restriction in countless ways. We may demand the novel be fiction, but many authors have woven reality and history into their novels for many reasons. We may ask that a novel be a prose narrative, but novels exists that contain rhythmic structure, either interspersed with prose text or in lieu of it. But in general the novel is a book, between one hundred and one thousand pages long, that tells a single story.

The best way to form a sense of what the novel is is to read one. Through varied exposure to novels you will begin to understand the shape of them, the thrust of their ambitions. You will forgive their indefinite nature, and come to appreciate the surprises offered by such creative freedom.

TYPES OF NOVELS

BILDUNGSROMAN
The "coming-of-age" novel is not a category you will find in any bookshop, but nevertheless remains one of the most popular and enduring genres of literature written. The growth of a protagonist from youth to adulthood is the essence of human storytelling.

e.g. *Portrait of the Artist as a Young Man,* by James Joyce

THE CRIME NOVEL
Crime novels are concerned with the act in all its forms: its execution, its detection, and its punishment. Many of the television programmes you watch today have their roots in crime novels, where long ago we discovered our fascination with the detective and the criminal mind. Murder is the ultimate, most ratifying puzzle.

e.g. *The Murder of Roger Ackroyd,* by Agatha Christie

THE HISTORICAL NOVEL
Historical context is crucial to many stories. The historical novel is concerned with known figures or events, either directly or tangentially. Many novels are set in past ages, however, and can be culturally illuminating even if the events portrayed are entirely or partially fictional.

e.g. *I, Claudius,* by Robert Graves

FIGURE 1: http://introducingthenovel.com

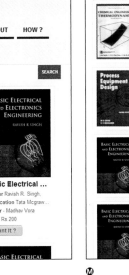

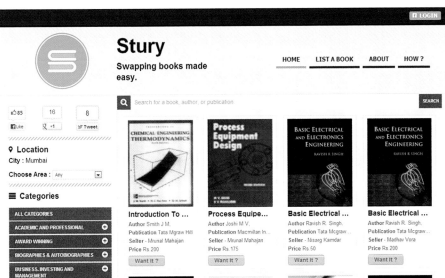

FIGURE 2: www.stury.in

We're a small studio. Small means more thought, care and attention to detail

Our team consists of experienced designers and programmers who all, want to make things that engage with people in positive ways.

It may be more than a little cliche to say 'Work hard, play hard' but surely playing with the latest technologies can't be classed as work when we love what we do. Passion is what drives or team; our passion for tackling meaty challenges, our passion for smart design and clever code, and our passion for having fun while creating solutions that we can feel proud of.

We're a small studio. Small means more thought, care and attention to detail

Our team consists of experienced designers and programmers who all, want to make things that engage with people in positive ways.

It may be more than a little cliche to say 'Work hard, play hard' but surely playing with the latest technologies can't be classed as work when we love what we do. Passion is what drives or team; our passion for tackling meaty challenges, our passion for smart design and clever code, and our passion for having fun while creating solutions that we can feel proud of.

Solving tough challenges demands a mix of people who can apply their expertise creatively. Our team come from a variety of industry backgrounds and experiences, yet we're all unified by a core value to make things that engage with people in positive ways. So if you're after a freshness and agility not found in larger agencies. We can help!

• WHAT WE DO •

| Strategy | Design | Development | Support |

Ⓜ

www.fiafo.com Ⓣ

Work **Info** Notes Shop

Hi, I'm Tyler Finck

ONLINE

Email
Zerply
Twitter
Instagram
Facebook

OFFLINE

+1 607 216 8779
P O Box 6776
Ithaca, NY 14850
USA

👍 82

ⓕ Like

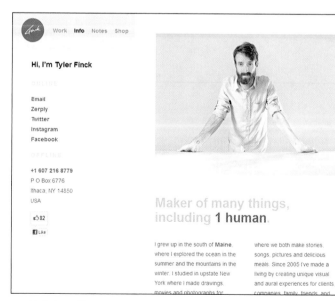

Maker of many things, including **1 human**.

I grew up in the south of **Maine**, where I explored the ocean in the summer and the mountains in the winter. I studied in upstate New York where I made drawings, movies and photographs for grades but never

Maker of many things, including **1 human**.

I grew up in the south of **Maine**, where I explored the ocean in the summer and the mountains in the winter. I studied in upstate New York where I made drawings, movies and photographs for

where we both make stories, songs, pictures and delicious meals. Since 2005 I've made a living by creating unique visual and aural experiences for clients companies, family, friends, and

Ⓜ

www.tylerfinck.com Ⓣ

www.lottanieminen.com

Learn from industry leading speakers.

Jeffrey Zeldman

Dubbed KING of Web Standards by Business Week. One of the first web designers, Zeldman has had a pronounced impact on the medium and the profession. In 1995, the former art director and copywriter launched one of the first personal sites and began publishing widely-read tutorials on methods and principles of web design.

Jonathan Stark

Jonathan Stark is a mobile consultant and web evangelist who believes that wireless computing will transform every aspect of society.

Jonathan is the author of three books on mobile and web development, most notably O'Reilly's Building iPhone Apps with HTML, CSS, and JavaScript which is available in seven languages.

Learn from industry leading speakers.

Jeffrey Zeldman

@zeldman

http://gobeyondpixels.com

Images

Of all the things we pack into sites, text and images are the most fundamental and unavoidable of elements. Here, I want to focus on the use of images in responsive design and how images might be adapted to fit various screen sizes. You may presume that images simply size up and down to fit screens, and this is one option. But there are other options available to the designer that offer up other perks.

As it turns out, there are really two core approaches to adapting images. The first, as stated above, is to simply size the images up and down. We find this on several examples, including the Bristol-Myers **(FIGURE 1)** and Charlotte Tang **(FIGURE 2)** websites. The images on these sites remain the same and simply shrink or grow to fit the needs of the layout. This, of course, implies a fundamental restriction that the designer must work with as the various sizes of the design are planned for.

The second option we have is to create images that contain fringe content that can be safely cropped off. In such cases, the sites use the same images across all screen sizes, but scale the containers they are in such that only part of the images show. Naturally, this means that these cropable pixels must be extra or supportive in nature. This is actually abundantly clear on the bronco.co.uk website **(FIGURE 3)**. Note how the tablet versions have images that are much wider and contain extra data, while on the phone version, the images are clipped off. Interestingly, the desktop version of the site uses the same image format as the phone one and demonstrates that careful planning can lead to extremely re-usable assets.

There is actually a third option, which I don't happen to have samples of, but I want to mention, if only to get you thinking. This option is to actually replace images to fit each layout. In this case, the code of the site could display one image for desktop users, a different one for tablets and a third for phone-based users. These three images are totally different image files, each optimized to the size and resolution of the display type they are intended for. This approach, in fact, is already used to swap out images for Retina and non-Retina displays and can easily be extended to support images targeted at particular screen dimensions.

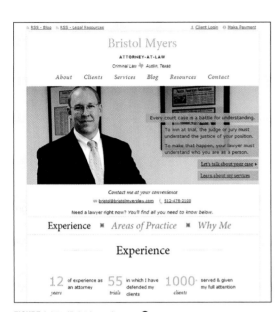

FIGURE 1: http://bristolmyerslaw.com ⬤   Ⓜ

FIGURE 2: http://charlottetang.com ⬤   Ⓜ

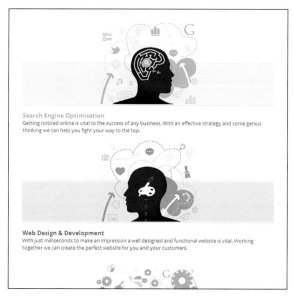

Search Engine Optimisation
Getting noticed online is vital to the success of any business. With an effective strategy and some genius thinking we can help you fight your way to the top.

Web Design & Development
With just milliseconds to make an impression a well designed and functional website is vital. Working together we can create the perfect website for you and your customers.

Search Engine Optimisation
Getting noticed online is vital to the success of any business. With an effective strategy and some genius thinking we can help you fight your way to the top.

Web Design & Development
With just milliseconds to make an impression a well designed and functional website is vital. Working together we can create the perfect website for you and your customers.

FIGURE 3: http://www.bronco.co.uk 🅣

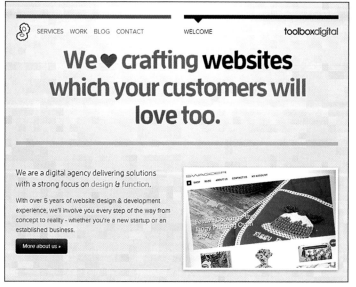

http://toolboxdigital.com 🅣

www.thestylejunkies.com **T**

M

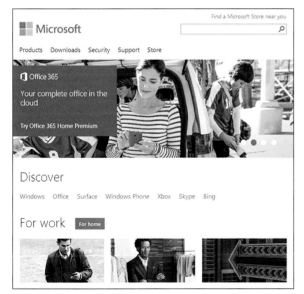

www.microsoft.com **T**

M

Maps

Implementing maps is super easy on the web; you just grab a bit of code and plug it into your site. However, two things remain relatively challenging: customizing maps visually and adapting them to fit various screen sizes. As such, the samples presented here stand out because they contain maps that are not only beautiful and functional, but also because they adapt so elegantly to a range of screen sizes.

One of my favorites is the contact page for Poolie Studios in Germany **(FIGURE 1)**. On this page, the map is a part of the background, though it is a fully functional Google map. Clearly the site's designers and developers didn't accept the default Google Maps styles. The colors and markers are all adapted to perfectly match the site's design. And more importantly, the space the map occupies naturally adapts to fit a full range of screen sizes.

Another interesting example that I believe illustrates a valuable point is the contact form on the Wise Design agency site **(FIGURE 2)**. Here, the map is again a functional and decorative element of the page. But note how the extra content (image and address) is laid on top of the map. In the responsive mobile version, this information and content is moved off of the map. The result is a simpler-to-use mobile interface that is not confused by content on top of a map. In fact, one might argue that on the phone version of the site, the map is even more important, as it is more likely someone is trying to find your office. In a simple way, this rearranging of the content is very practical.

Finally, I want to turn your attention to the site of Will McMahan **(FIGURE 3)**. It reminds us that at times maps are informational, but need not be functional. The location of the individual is clearly established, but we don't need to be able to navigate to his house or office. As a result, this image-based solution is easier to style to match the site and far easier to adapt to various layouts.

While maps may be a challenging technical element, they don't necessarily have to be overly complicated on responsive layouts. Work with your developer to see what is possible and you may be pleasantly surprised.

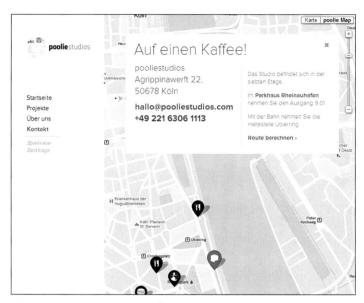
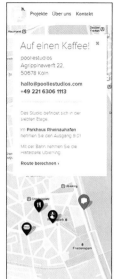

FIGURE 1: http://pooliestudios.com/kontakt

FIGURE 2: www.wise-digital.com/contact

FIGURE 3: http://wmcmahan.com Ⓣ

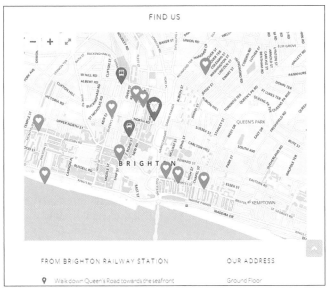

http://builtbybuffalo.com/contact Ⓣ

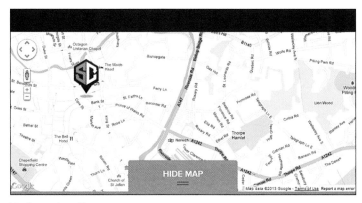

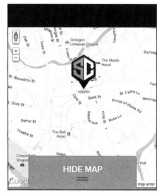

http://syncconf.com 🅣

🅜

http://welcomedavid.se 🅣

🅜

Footers

Of all the elements presented here, the footer is perhaps among the easiest to address. In so many cases, the content is so simple that adapting it is not much of a challenge. In others, it is quite often about hiding and removing extra bits on smaller devices. Despite this simplistic view, let's dissect a few examples to discover how we might tackle this page-ending element.

In some cases a footer can be so simple that it need not change at all. Take Jet Cooper, for example **(FIGURE 1)**. Here the footer contains but two links: a logo and a copyright statement. And, as you can see when the screen shrinks down, there is simply no need to change the layout! This definitely falls into the category of not over-complicating something. Keep it simple—and if the content is this simple, don't create extra work for yourself.

In contrast, the footer found on the Acorn Independent Mortgages website contains a fair amount of content that does require special attention **(FIGURE 2)**. In this case, the footer contains three columns of content that conveniently stack on top of each other. If the site is built on a responsive framework, this likely came into being with almost no effort on the developer's part.

In other cases, like the Sasquatch Festival website, **(FIGURE 3)** some elements of a footer can be hidden as the screen size decreases. Here the playlist feature is removed and hidden on small screens. We also find this strategy at work on the HealthLife website **(FIGURE 4)**, where the logo is hidden on smaller screens. It seems that this repeated bit of content simply isn't necessary on small devices. Hiding the logo might at first sound unthinkable, but it works really well in this case. The moral of the story is to not think of each element as sacred, but instead look at each one objectively to determine how to handle it.

Finally, I want to focus on the Charming Inns website, as it illustrates a point I would like to make **(FIGURE 5)**. On tablets and desktops this site footer contains two large lists of links in horizontal rows. This fits these devices nicely and works well. Transition to the phone version and you will notice that one of these lists takes a purely vertical approach, while the other simply wraps to multiple lines. I would argue that the first list is more important and thus justifies the larger amount of space it occupies. Meanwhile, the second list is less important and is visually condensed. The second list is actually rather difficult to use unless you zoom in on your phone. I suspect that the site's designers are well aware of this, and in this case I am 100% on board with their decision. These elements are simply not core to the function of the site, and making someone work a bit to get them feels just fine to me.

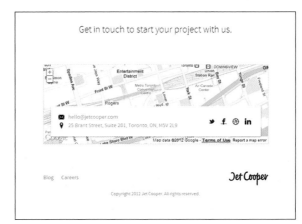

FIGURE 1: www.jetcooper.com

FIGURE 2: www.acorn4mortgages.co.uk

FIGURE 3: www.sasquatchfestival.com

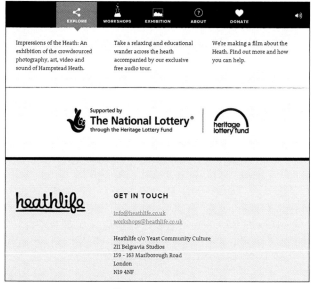

FIGURE 4: http://heathlife.co.uk

FIGURE 5: www.wentworthmansion.com **T**

www.printgr.am **T**

05

Design Styles

When it comes to web design, styles change rapidly. At any given time we can find a tremendous range of styles in use, but there always seems to be a predominant style that tends to stand out. As I have written my Idea Books over the years, it is interesting to look back and see how each book emerged during a distinct stylistic period. Each of these styles fades in popular use, and instead finds a place in the designer's tool belt as a resource to solve specific visual problems. With this in mind, I want to start the design styles section with four of the most prominent current approaches, which happens to include one outlier that actually works against the trends to stand out in a unique way.

Super Clean

One design style that I have showcased in every one of my Idea Books is Super Clean (also known as Ultra Clean in Idea Book, Volume 2). As I have so often said, this section almost always includes my absolute favorite examples, and oftentimes demonstrates the best of the best. It also tends to contain a nice array of sites that vividly demonstrate an ability to be timeless. Case in point: if you look back to Idea Book, Volume 1, you would find that at least 50 percent of the sites presented there would fit nicely into the modern web. Let's dive in and look at some examples.

Frankly speaking, I was surprised when I stumbled upon this micro site put out by Vogue **(FIGURE 1)**. What you find here is a design that is insanely streamlined. It is minimal in so many ways, and yet feels far more decorative than it is. The prominent images carry the design and one thing I really love is the vertical cropping of the images. After all, photos of models showcasing clothing fit this format perfectly. And the side-by-side images are a brilliantly simple solution. Finally, I really love that their large block of text with a call to action overlaps the images and gives the design depth. It can be so tempting to simply stack things up. Sometimes a little overlap goes a long way in creating visual interest and controlling a user's attention.

Another site I simply fell in love with was the Etch site **(FIGURE 2)**. This extremely clean design is easy on the eyes and well organized. While most decorative elements have been removed and the design embodies a minimalistic approach, it feels anything but minimal. It just feels super clean and simply gorgeous. Though the MapBox site **(FIGURE 3)** is not reversed out in the same way, it feels very similar to the Etch site in that it is so extremely refined. If you are looking for beautiful sites to emulate, you would be hard pressed to pick better examples than one of these two.

Finally, I want to highlight the Dust and Mold Design website **(FIGURE 4)**. This chapter can start to feel limited to sites embracing a minimal approach, but that is not entirely the case. This site, for example, easily fits into the super clean category, and it is anything but minimal. Instead, it clearly embodies the ideas core to this topic. The design is extremely refined, the content is easy to consume, and the layout is free of all unneeded clutter.

FIGURE 1: www.vogue.co.uk Ⓜ

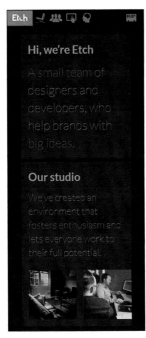

FIGURE 2: http://etchapps.com Ⓜ

FIGURE 3: http://mapbox.com Ⓜ

FIGURE 4: http://dustandmold.net Ⓜ

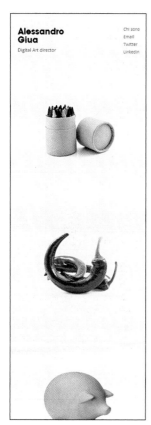

Alessandro Giua
Digital Art director

Chi sono
Email
Twitter
LinkedIn

= MENU

HEY, I'M MATTHEW CARLETON A PASSIONATE DESIGNER WHO HAPPENS TO BE FOR SALE

★ hire me

I'M ONE OF THOSE DESIGNERS WHO IS COMPLETELY OBSESSED WITH THE WEB.

I've been designing & building web sites for over five years now & can't seem to get enough of it. I spend my days working for clients & my nights working on personal projects like Huurd & Designers Blueprint. I am constantly honing my craft, learning new methods & trends, I am never satisfied. I write now and then, check out my latest article Sites of the Week 8: Some Personal Inspiration.

I live in Halifax, Nova Scotia with my stunning wife. I have a list of great clients both near & far. I am always seeking new projects that are both exciting & challenging. If you are in need of branding,

RR Rockaway Relief ≡

The Rockaways Are Devastated and They Need Your Help.

RSVP TO VOLUNTEER

The Situation
CURRENT STATE OF THE ROCKAWAYS

The peninsula situated along the Atlantic Ocean in the borough of Queens was devastated by a large storm surge from Hurricane Sandy this October.

big.com   Agence de communication experte en innovation digitale   Menu

A la une

Citroën : Ecosystème Citroën.com

Les derniers Case Studies

Thierry Mugler : Dispositif digital international pour les 20 ans du parfum Angel
Big Youth a été retenu par les parfums Thierry Mugler pour travailler sur des opérations digitales. Première collaboration et premier enjeu : comment célébrer les 20 ans de la marque Angel sur le digital ?
Détail

http://touchtech.co.nz

www.hanskfroschauer.com

www.techdept.co.uk

http://diglondon.ca

Flat Pixels

One of the most prominent design trends at the time of this writing is known as Flat Pixels. I first saw the term on the blog of Sacha Greif, where he has a rather extensive description and analysis of the style and its roots[1]. While I will give a brief overview of the concept here, I do encourage you to check out his more extensive analysis.

Flat pixels is essentially the polar opposite of skeuomorph-based design. Skeuomorphism is when a design relies on visual decoration that relates to the object in the real world. A prime example is the calendar built into the iPad: It features a leather texture and stitching that connects with real-life calendars. It is not necessary for the design onscreen, except to help establish the purpose of the application. In some cases skeumorphs are used for more practical purposes, but the relationship to the real world item is always there.

In stark contrast, flat pixels is a rejection of this and instead focuses on extremely simplified and flat designs. While skeumorphs often lead to 3-D-like interfaces, flat pixel-based designs lack the visual depths. Interestingly, the newest mobile devices feature super high-resolution displays (like the Apple Retina display). On these sites, simpler interfaces like this actually highlight the quality of the display better then a visually rich one does. It is counterintuitive but very true.

A perfect example of this is the TinyLetter website **(FIGURE 1)**. Here, the flat design is simply gorgeous. It allows the content to shine, and the design is supportive of the purpose of the site. Interestingly the main call to action has a hint of 3-D styling to it. In this way, the site subtly breaks the pattern and forces the most important element of the page to pop out. As is often the case, a much more restrained design creates the opportunity to showcase prominent elements in far more subtle ways. The real point though, is that we need not stick to any style religiously and can intermix them for powerful results.

In case you're worried that a flat design equates to a boring one, I want to direct your attention to the Flavor website **(FIGURE 2)**. Here the design is certainly flat, but far from boring. Instead the design is incredibly distinct, rather beautiful and though the design is decorative, it quickly brings you back to the core content.

---

[1] http://sachagreif.com/flat-pixels

FIGURE 1: http://tinyletter.com

We're a digital studio passionate about design and technology.

We dream big and work hard to create beautiful, engaging experiences.

Interested in working with us?
hello@weareflavor.com

Want to know our favorite ice cream?
@weareflavor

FIGURE 2: www.weareflavor.com

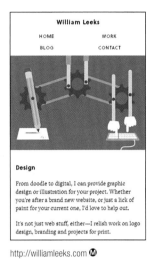

Design

From doodle to digital, I can provide graphic design or illustration for your project. Whether you're after a brand new website, or just a lick of paint for your current one, I'd love to help out.

It's not just web stuff, either—I relish work on logo design, branding and projects for print.

http://williamleeks.com

www.reamaze.com

http://alphalab.org

http://mapbox.com

www.elliotcondon.com

http://jimramsden.com

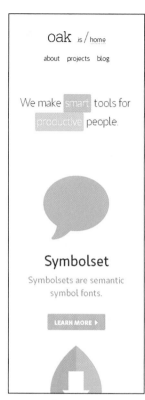

http://oak.is

http://builtbyboon.com

www.sicky.net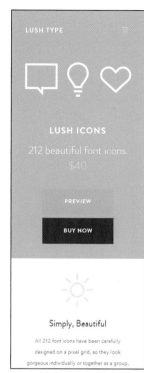

www.lushtype.com

Decorative

Oftentimes when I am describing trends or patterns I love to contradict myself. And this is exactly what I want to do in this chapter. These decorative designs buck the trend toward flat pixels and lean toward more decorative or elaborate designs. Before I dive in, I do want to address what you're likely thinking: "You call these decorative?" I know these designs don't feel all that ornate. In fact, if you look back to my first Idea Book you will find some chapters on ornate design that make these look minimal. The thing is that on the mobile web these are actually rather decorative. By decorative, I mean they rely on designs that contain lots of extra decoration that creates a distinct look and feel. In a way, it really is kind of funny that this is what qualifies as decorative on the mobile web, but after looking at many thousands of sites I stand by my assessment.

I believe there are two reasons this approach is so seldom used. First, with responsive design, it is really complicated to adapt a site to many different screen sizes. As a result, designers have gravitated toward minimal, streamlined designs, as they are simply easier to adapt. Second, on mobile devices we tend to be more concerned with load speeds and therefore lean toward cleaner and simpler designs that load less decorative "stuff."

One of my favorites here is the Sweet Hat Club website **(FIGURE 1)**. This delicious site is by no means overly decorative. In fact, I would say the decoration used on the site fits brilliantly with the content of the site. It has just enough decoration to resonate with the topic, and yet is streamlined enough that the design doesn't slow the site down. A very nice balance between practical issues and design-based messaging is found here.

Another example that demonstrates that decorative doesn't mean overdoing it on the mobile web is iwantedrock.com **(FIGURE 2)**. On the desktop, this site feels anything but decorative. But in the mobile context it is not the norm and feels far more decorative than you might suspect. The Station Street restaurant site **(FIGURE 3)** also fits neatly into this category. On the mobile web it feels downright visually intense, but on desktops it is nearly minimal.

Frankly speaking, I think this is an area ripe with opportunity. While I am by no means encouraging designers to build over-the-top obnoxious designs, if you do happen to build some decorative elements into your design, it can give your site a distinct look. If all mobile sites are streamlined and minimal, they will start to blend together. In fact, as a whole, the contents of this book feel far less diverse when compared to one of my previous Idea Books. This is entirely due to the streamlining of sites for the mobile web, and again, this presents designers with the opportunity to introduce some distinctive decoration.

FIGURE 1: http://sweethatclub.org

FIGURE 2: http://iwantedrock.com

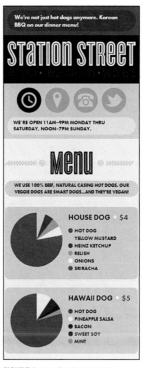

FIGURE 3: http://stationstreetpgh.com

http://dangelicoguitars.com

www.journeyofthemouse.com Ⓜ

www.flite.com Ⓜ

http://rypearts.com Ⓜ

http://ovenbits.com Ⓜ

Majestic Turkish Coffee

Did you know that Turkish coffee consists of an extra fine grind mixed with sugar and water? You can also add orange blossom water or spices such as cardamom.

Photo credits

What's happening now?

All   Friends

Nathalie will try Who Wants to Be a Barista?

Solange wowed Time for the Perfect Cup of Coffee

Sylvie will try Lovely Days Start With Café au Lait

Nathalie wowed Beauty & the Beans

https://yournow.ca/van-houtte-now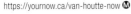

Lincoln Arts Project presents The National Poster Retrospecticus, a collection of hand-printed posters from over 50 local,

http://nationalposterretrospecticus.com Ⓜ

http://buildguild.org Ⓜ

Hi, I'm Meagan Fisher, a designer in New York City. I make websites, eat food, & love owls.

Things that I am excited about

There's been so much going on behind the scenes at Owltastic that I've predictably dropped the ball on writing over the last month. But May is upon us! Maybe it's time for an Ideas of May initiative. In the meantime, here's a few things I've been up to these last few weeks:

http://owltastic.com Ⓜ

Minimal

If ever there's a default design style to fall back on, it is definitely minimalism. And this is even more true on the mobile web where minimalism is perhaps your most useful asset. The minimal approach plays nice on the mobile web for so many reasons, so let's consider a few of the key highlights. Minimal sites tend to have smaller file sizes due to the streamlined design. Minimal sites can more easily adapt to various layouts via responsive techniques as there's less stuff to deal with—it tends to just be a matter of mashing the content around. On the mobile web you have small screens and short attention spans and minimalistic mindsets help you get to the point quickly. A well-executed minimal site has the tendency to feel slick and is a timeless approach. This will help increase the shelf life of your site and reduce your long-term costs. All of these are substantial reasons to go with this style.

Notebook Media **(FIGURE 1)** is a website based on minimalistic styles and it serves as a perfect sample for this chapter. Clearly the site is void of structural decorations that frame or contain things. Instead, the design is wide open, allowing the text and images to form the spaces. I am fascinated with how content alone can provide more than enough structure for a site. I also appreciate the fact that the site's designers didn't feel it necessary to religiously stick with minimalism. In fact, I bet they didn't even think of it in that way. I imagine they just removed everything they didn't need and put a high polish on what was left. Never let this style lull you into thinking that it is easy. Ironically, it is much harder to design with less than it is with more.

I find that the Palantir site **(FIGURE 2)** is an interesting demonstration of the style as well. Again, the minimalist mindset isn't extreme and the end product is certainly not a strictly minimal design. And this real-world result is exactly why I love looking at actual websites and not textbook examples. What makes me call this one out though, is how they have woven their personal style into the site. You will no doubt notice the prominent illustration. Granted, it isn't visible until you scroll down the page a bit, but still the overall style of the page is clearly their own. This, of course, is one potential pitfall of sticking too closely to a purely minimal design; that you somehow lose any personal touches and become an altogether forgettable design. Naturally, I don't believe any of the samples here fall into this trap.

Notebook Media is a small team of designers & developers that will bring your ideas and concepts to life.

WORK

FIGURE 1: http://notebookmedia.com ⓜ

---

palantir.net

Services   Team   Work

Blog   Contact

EXPLORING ONLINE SPACE

Our mission at Palantir® is to empower and enable people everywhere to share information through highly functional websites and interactive software.

FIGURE 2: www.palantir.net ⓜ

CODES DESIGN FURNITURES PHOTOSTREAM

PEACH MONROE
Design

CODES
Scripts for websites

VALIDATA
Tuesday 10 July 2012, 0.56

(Italiano) Ultimamente ho cercato in rete un plug-in per jQuery che mi potesse aiutare con la validazione dei campi durante la compilazione di un form HTML, tuttavia quelli che ho trovato non mi hanno soddisfatto pienamente, così ho deciso di scriverne uno che potesse essere versatile e adatto in tutte le situazioni in cui sono abituato a lavorare… ➡

http://vittoriovittori.com/en ⓜ

GARETH LAWN
PRINT & WEB DESIGN

HOME PORTFOLIO BLOG

Hello, welcome to the online home of print and web designer, **Gareth Lawn**. Based in North Wales, I work largely in print design but I'm delving more and more into the weird but wonderful world of web development.

Uncle Chops Smokehouse Branding
Client: Uncle Chops Smokehouse *Type of work:* Branding

Read more »

LLANDUDNO
ESPLANADE
HOTEL & RESTAURANT

Esplanade Hotel Branding
Client: Esplanade Hotel
Type of work: Branding

http://garethlawn.co.uk ⓜ

Three reasons to be jolly

Bring the holiday treats

www.starbucks.com ⓜ

Web design

We create completely bespoke, striking designs that work alongside your brand to engage and enthral your target audience. Clarity is key.

Web development

We integrate cutting edge content management and e-commerce systems, develop mobile applications and other technical stuff.

Content Strategy

We take the time to understand what it is you want to say and help you develop copy that is engaging and informative.

Read more

http://builtwithmomentum.com ⓜ

Hello, my name is Simon Foster and I run a tiny one-man web design studio in London, England. I specialise in responsive front-end design, HTML/CSS and web typography. I try to make the websites I design and build as simple and intuitive to use as possible whilst still having a unique aesthetic appeal. Please feel free to have a look at the work in my portfolio, or if you like, check out some of my side projects and resources. My work is regularly featured in all kinds of design

http://simonfosterdesign.com/home ⓜ

We make digital products to improve people's lives.

We invent digital products to express the natural character of our true human relationships. Think of things that light you up. Someone you love, a conversation, a perfect song. Now imagine new ways to capture these moments. What are they like? Can we make them? Let's try.

We help others invent digital products by offering our expertise and resources as both service and investment. Our integrated approach consists of strategy, cultural research, branding, content, design and technology. A digital partner for the world's best and brightest.

http://crushlovely.com ⓜ

Elliot Jay Stocks is a designer, speaker, and author. He is one half of Viewport Industries and the founder of typography magazine 8 Faces.

Home   Blog   Speaking   About

Quatro

Posted on 13 December 2012

I've had a very personal relationship with Quatro (Sans / Slab) for a number of years now. I loved its first incarnation — the Ultra weight of the Sans — and when I came to do the branding for Brooklyn Beta, I was able to use the then-beta (see what I did there) version of Quatro Slab, thanks to the generosity of designer Mark Caneso. Over the years, Mark and I have become friends, and in that space of time he's expanded both the Sans and Slab from Ultras to full, multi-weight families.

http://elliotjaystocks.com

Publications   Online

Events   Books

Dental Publications, Websites and Events

Get to know FMC

Latest News:

http://www.fmc.co.uk

Dr. Bischoff & Tann

Navigate to...

WIR BIETEN BESTE BERATUNG.

Wir nehmen uns die Zeit jeden einzelnen Klienten zu verstehen, deshalb arbeiten wir hart daran individuelle Strategien für jeden Kunden zu entwickeln.

INTERNATIONALE STEUERBERATUNG

Aufgrund unserer guten Kontakte zu einer in Hamburg ansässigen, europaweit tätigen Gesellschaft, ...

MEHR ERFAHREN

www.b-and-t.de

robertsonuk.net
simple websites for nice people

man in a **shed**

maninashed.co.uk
nicer than you thought

Andrea Willans

andreawillans.co.uk
she was 'made-up'

http://www.robertsonuk.net

Color Block

The use of solid color blocks as a design element makes perfect sense in the mobile world. Much like the minimal style, it is bandwidth-friendly and extremely flexible for responsive design. Another way the two styles are similar is that they both look deceptively easy. I have actually attempted this approach several times, and to my frustration, I have had sub-par results. On a personal level, I find the sites here a tad annoying (as well as inspiring) for this very reason—the designers have pulled the style off in such vivid and beautiful ways.

The website for Somewhat **(FIGURE 1)** is a prime example of this. The end result here is just outstanding, with the obvious use of solid color regions. Two small details stand out to me and really seem to make the site. First is the gradient approach to the series of links. This approach breaks up the list and gives the page an interesting style as it transitions from header and links to content. It's a classic example of an idea you find yourself annoyed you didn't think of. Next up is the gradient-mapped photo in the header. By transforming this photo into a single color range, it fits into the solid color approach, meaning that it matches the other elements of the page beautifully. A black and white version might have worked here, but it wouldn't have given the page the pop that the yellow version does. The results are envy-worthy, to say the least.

Let's change our focus to another sample, the Fiafo website **(FIGURE 2)** . We of course see an abundance of solid-colored regions, but the whole site is fantastic, and one detail in particular pushes it over the top—the typography. The type on this page is just beautiful. The combination of fonts works so well and the various type elements have been beautifully crafted. This is perhaps the real driving force in the design. The solid colors are merely there to support it and give accent.

On the Clean Air Works site **(FIGURE 3)**, we see another technique using solid colors that I believe is worth mentioning. Notice how the various elements—icons, text, support illustrations, buttons, etc.—all make use of the style. In a world of CSS3 gradients and drop shadows it can be tempting to weave them in unnecessarily. By staying away from these, the site has a vividly unified style that is supported by the use of solid colors and the total lack of anything otherwise.

FIGURE 1: www.somewhat.cc

FIGURE 2: www.fiafo.com

FIGURE 3: http://clearairchallenge.com

www.aptify.com

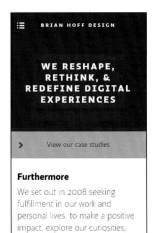

Furthermore

We set out in 2008 seeking fulfillment in our work and personal lives: to make a positive impact, explore our curiosities,

www.brianhoffdesign.com

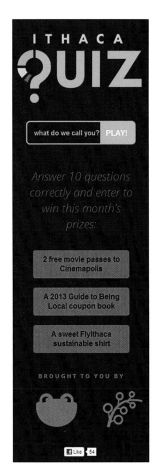

www.ithacaquiz.com

www.microsoft.com/en-us/default. aspx

www.buildwindows.com

Skip to Navigation
Skip to Content

Follow us on Twitter

digitalhappy
think · create · support

home

our company & services

our portfolio

contact us

We use our creative design and development skills to produce web sites and print designs that are well conceived, look great and are expertly put together.

We love what we do and provide great results for our clients' projects. So if you're looking for effective, cost-efficient solutions for your digital media needs, have a look at our work and get in touch.

Latest digitalHappy news

www.digitalhappy.com

DON'T TALK TO ROBOTS

PORTFOLIO **ABOUT** **CONTACT**

Creating experiences that

COMMUNICATE WITH PEOPLE.

Don't Talk to Robots, the portfolio of designer and developer Doug Vander Meulen.

PORTFOLIO

Hope Renewed

http://donttalktorobots.com

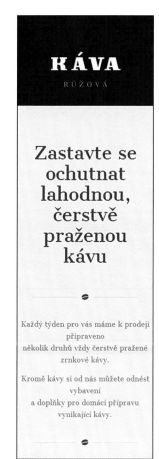

KÁVA

RŮŽOVÁ

Zastavte se ochutnat lahodnou, čerstvě praženou kávu

Každý týden pro vás máme k prodeji připraveno
několik druhů vždy čerstvě pražené zrnkové kávy.

Kromě kávy si od nás můžete odnést vybavení
a doplňky pro domácí přípravu vynikající kávy.

www.kavaruzova.cz

gravitate

HOME WORK SERVICES COMPANY BLOG
CONTACT

Business is looking up... will yours be ready?

Savvy businesses armed with the right strategy and design will be poised to take full advantage of an economic uptick. Let us help you build your arsenal.

Our Work

WORK

Tamarack

As a custom home builder, Tamarack wanted to ensure its marketing presence matched the high-end

www.gravitatedesign.com

Atypical Layouts

One design style that I have featured in each volume of the *Web Designer's Idea Books* is that of atypical layouts. It seems that no matter how often the industry agrees on ways of designing things, there are always designers out there that manage to bend and adapt the web to do extremely unique things. The result is a set of sites that go together only because they are all so distinct and different. These sites are often among the most inspiring.

A perfect example to start with is Photoshop Etiquette **(FIGURE 1)**. Browse the site on your mobile device and you will feel right at home. It's comfortable and easy to use. The message is clear; the product is easy to understand. That said, the site has a rather distinct flavor. Like so many other mobile sites, it relies on a vertical column of text. But if you dissect it further you will notice that the layout is not the norm.

The website for Niedlov's Breadworks **(FIGURE 2)** also pushes the boundaries and questions how things must be presented. Here, we see a series of large images that communicate the site's purpose and provide a portal to additional content. It seems to me that many sites on the mobile web blend together. A site like this that presents such a distinct and unique approach is far more memorable—and yet remains easy to use. Maintaining a delicate balance between being atypical and usable is crucial to the success of a website. The upside can be powerful though, and is often worth the extra work.

Another, more radical example I really appreciate is I Am Ousbäck **(FIGURE 3)**. The layout is completely beyond what you might expect. What I can't help noticing about this example is how they keep it usable. The site doesn't follow the norms, but to counter this, it is so streamlined that it is really hard to be confused about using it. I think there is a lot of wisdom in this. If your site pushes the boundaries and doesn't adhere to the norms, you should carefully consider a streamlined interface that helps minimize confusion.

FIGURE 1: http://photoshopetiquette.com

FIGURE 2: http://niedlovs.com Ⓜ

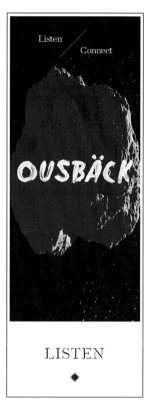

FIGURE 3: www.iamousback.com Ⓜ

http://moderngreenhome.com Ⓜ

http://keynesforkids.com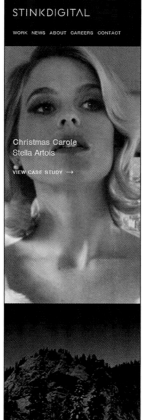

www.stinkdigital.com

http://shinydemos.com

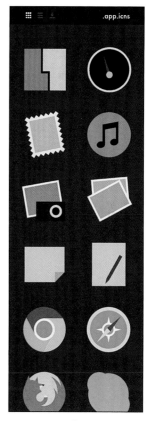

http://appicns.com

BIO SKILLS WORK OTHERS CONTACT

HI THERE
I'm Peter

WEB & GRAPHIC DESIGNER
HTML/CSS CODER
WORDPRESS DEVELOPER
CREATIVE GUY

BIO
Life of Peter

1978 — CHILDHOOD

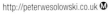

http://peterwesolowski.co.uk

OKUMA

Thank you for visiting the Okuma Corporate Global Home Page. Please select the region where you reside and learn about how Okuma can solve your most challenging production machining problems with the most advanced machine tools in the world.

Europe & Africa

THE AMERICAS

JAPAN
- JAPANESE
- ENGLISH
- CHINESE

ASIA
- CHINA
- INDIA
- TAIWAN
- SOUTH EAST ASIA
- OTHER ASIAN OFFICES

AUSTRALIA & NEW ZEALAND

EUROPE & AFRICA

www.okuma.com

Catalysis. Organometallic chemistry.

Research and Study at the School of Chemistry

We are based in the Synthetic Chemistry Building of the School of Chemistry with unrivalled...

Find out more

Dr Dowson

www.wassresearchgroup.com

CLIENTS

Afflatus Project
Agora
American Board of Internal Medicine
American Express
AmerisourceBergen
Artisan Garden
Barrett N Smith
Bixler's Jewelers
Blessing Health System
Blue Mountain Health System
Bom Magazine
Caretech Connectivity
Caretech Solutions Presentation
Carpenter Technology
CASPA
Cellphone Art - Start Mobile
Centegra Health System
Checkpoint Systems
Children's Discovery Institute
Children's Hospital, New Orleans

www.jonjon.tv

Typography

As designers, typography is something we are always interested in. On the mobile web, a lot of focus is placed on streamlining things so they load fast. As a result it seems that custom typography is often overlooked. However, as you will see in the samples here, the mobile web can still be a place to find beautiful typography.

Though text in images is a bit out of style, it is still an extremely viable option. Getting images to work at various sizes is a hurdle that can take some work to accommodate for. Overcome both of these obstacles and you may find beautiful sites like Hundredth Monkey **(FIGURE 1)** . Here, the large decorative type is displayed in an image and looks gorgeous on mobile devices. I really love that this decorative element also does a great job at communicating with the visitor. The text draws you in and gets you curious about their services. With all the streamlining that happens to make sites mobile-friendly, we can all too easily lose the core elements that make our site and brand stand out. In this case the shop's voice, style and brand carry through to mobile.

In many of the other samples, we find that the headings and content have been lovingly styled so as to be easy to read and to clearly establish the hierarchy of the content. Samples like the Harpeth Valley Animal Hospital **(FIGURE 2)** and Upperdog **(FIGURE 3)** all stand out as examples where the basic text structure is just outstanding.

One sample that has interesting typography and stands out is the Meltmedia website **(FIGURE 4)**, where subtle changes in emphasis help the page to communicate in a radically fast way. Of all the samples here, I found this one to be one of the easiest to quickly take in and understand. Given how users scan content, it makes sense to ensure that the key words stand out. As simple an idea as this is, I actually think it is one of the most inspiring nuggets that can be absorbed from this section.

Finally, I wanted to point out the header text on Zach Woomer's site **(FIGURE 5)**. The text is bold and serves well as a page heading. But what I really appreciate about it is how the decoration and style of the text adds to the beauty of the page. The actual text is styled in such a way that it is beautiful and is not in need of supportive decoration. It is such a simple idea, yet so powerful. The decorated type gives the page beauty and style and helps it to remain lean and fast.

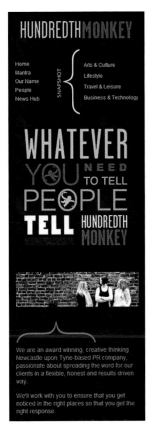

WHATEVER YOU NEED TO TELL PEOPLE TELL HUNDREDTH MONKEY

We are an award winning, creative thinking Newcastle upon Tyne-based PR company, passionate about spreading the word for our clients in a flexible, honest and results driven way.

We'll work with you to ensure that you get noticed in the right places so that you get the right response.

FIGURE 1: www.hundredthmonkeyuk.com

We offer the absolute best in health & wellness care.

Harpeth Valley Animal Hospital is a full service animal hospital that takes great pride in customer service and patient care.

Learn more about our services

FIGURE 2: http://hvanimalhospital.com Ⓜ

UPPERDOG

Vi är en webbyrå som skapar fantastiska webbplatser med genomtänkt strategi, design och funktion. Ring oss →

Strategi

Alla stora beslut bör fattas baserat på fakta – webbprojekt är inget undantag. Genom att förstå kunden och målgruppen, problem och möjligheter ser vi till att varje aspekt av webbplatsen jobbar mot samma mål. Läs mer →

Design

Design handlar inte om snyggt eller fult, utan om att lösa problem på ett kreativt sätt. Genom bra design skapar vi webbplatser som är tydliga, enkla att använda och som leder till fler avslut. Att det ser snyggt ut ser vi som en bonus. Läs mer →

Utveckling

Vi älskar teknik men förstår om du har annat att tänka på. Genom att utgå ifrån dina behov när vi väljer teknik får du en lösning som kostar dig mindre tid och pengar och som är lättare att underhålla och vidareutveckla. Läs mer →

FIGURE 3: http://upperdog.se Ⓜ

FIGURE 4: http://meltmedia.com Ⓜ

INFO   ARCHIVES   PROJECTS

FEAR AND LOATHING IN THE MOLESKIN

I'm on my third gin and tonic, feverishly scratching pencil to paper. Focused. The sounds of the music nothing but blobs of noise filling the room. Make a line, erase a line, make a line, erase a line, the art teeter-tottering out of me. I need a break, I need to stand. My back is beginning to feel like too much food on the end of a spoon.

I make my way to the kitchen. I need more gin fuel, unleaded. Midway back to my room I stop at the window. The night is still, corpse like. The filthy drunk bar pigs have already cleared the streets, made their way back to their pens.

Back to the desk now, back to my work. I run my hands through my hair habitually, knead my forehead, wipe off my clammy hands, repeat. I'm so close

FIGURE 5: www.zachwoomer.com

create

Home About Work Blog Jobs Contact

The art & science of app creation

`Creativity`

Where we're based

We're based in the beautiful town of Tunbridge Wells in Kent, England where we design apps for amazing clients worldwide.

What we do

We design beautiful, simple and highly functional apps for iPhone, iPad & Android. Check out our latest work.

http://createdm.com

HEY-HO@THILOTHAMM.COM

THILO THAMM

»I love digital. As a User Experience Designer I think of websites, interfaces, apps, and mobile«

KLOSTER PFORTA

all concept + design + code for the wineyards corporate website
- **onlineshop • microsites**
- kloster-pforta.de
- kloster-pforta.de/shop

www.thilothamm.com

SWISSSS

Home About Portfolio Blog
Friends Contact

THE CREATIVE PROCESS IS SUPPOSED TO BE THE FUN PART. ENJOY IT.

Not even smiled yet. Emotion by numbers, not funny, gurning face. Dire.

www.swissss.me

CITY CRAWLERS *BERLIN*

THE BOOK   PURCHASE   NEWS   PRESS   CONTACT

THE SEARCH TO FIND NEW PATTERNS,
BEHAVIORS, EXCEPTIONS AND BEAUTIFUL
FACTS THROUGH INFORMATION

NEWS & UPDATES

The Information
Architecture of Cities

Cities can be viewed as information
architecture systems. The term makes sense
not in reference to the the design of buildings,
but rather to the components of a complex
system that interact with each other. In a
paper…

January 3, 2011   *Read More*

Berlin Open Data
Hackathon

We're organizing the Berlin edition of the
global Open Data Hackathon. It will happen
on December 4th and starts at 09:30 in the
office of Your Neighbours, at the
Adalbertstrasse number 5 in Berlin. If you are
into…

November 29, 2010   *Read More*

Berlin Open Data

We are currently reviewing the data offered
by the city of Berlin. The results
are surprisingly good. Even though open data
in Germany isn't as widely available as it is in
some other european countries like Iceland…

August 22, 2010   *Read More*

http://citycrawlers.eu/berlin

EARTH HOUR
60 MINUTES POUR LA PLANÈTE

Samedi 23 mars 2013
de 20h30 à 21h30

ÉTEIGNONS LA LUMIÈRE POUR
VOIR LE MONDE AUTREMENT !

REGARDEZ LA VIDÉO ▶

ÉLUS, ENGAGEZ VOTRE VILLE

Le 31 mars, rejoignez le mouvement et engagez
votre ville dans la lutte contre le réchauffement
climatique.

ENGAGEZ-VOUS

CITOYENS, MOBILISEZ VOUS

Vous avez tous un rôle à jouer dans la lutte
contre le changement climatique.

MOBILISEZ-VOUS

http://earthhour.fr

www.codalight.com

Codalight créé
votre site internet
pour 450€ suivant
un processus
simplifié.

1

Choix du thème

Nous sélectionnons pour
vous une liste de thèmes
adaptée à votre activité.

C'est vous qui choisissez
celui que vous souhaitez.

www.codalight.com

cage

FEATURES   PRICING   CUSTOMERS

A simple way for designers
and teams to share,
manage and approve their
creative work.

Getting feedback and
your work approved
doesn't have to be
hard. See how we
make it easier.

http://cageapp.com

Type as Design

Typography on the web is an extremely hot topic that designers are fully embracing. As someone who has been building sites for a reasonably long time (since around 1999), it is indeed a very exciting time. For so long we have been stuck with such limited sets of type, it is truly exciting to experience the freedom we now have. The previous chapter focused on web typography, as does this chapter: Though they are very much interconnected, here I want to offer up a slightly different perspective on type. (Granted, a part of me just really loves the topic, and this allows me to indulge that interest.)

Here I want to consider type as a decorative part of a design. With responsive and mobile web design, a lot of emphasis has been placed on streamlining things. This means that on many websites, there is little in the way of decorative design. This leaves the work of beautifying a design to the text in the page. Fortunately, this is an area many designers excel and it is an opportunity to put those skills to work. Let's take a look at some samples to see exactly what I mean.

First, consider the Forge and Smith website **(FIGURE 1)**. This site is essentially built on solid blocks of color that help break the content up, but don't provide much in the way of style or decoration. In an extremely elegant way, the text-based logo/header provides the primary source of style on the page. It sets the tone and style for the page and reveals the agency's solid design skills. I am really amazed at how powerful such a small element can be. The real beauty of type is that it is always informative but can also be decorative.

Another lovely example of this is *The Shape of Design* book website **(FIGURE 2)**. In this case, the site has absolutely nothing in the way of decorative structural elements; just a simple solid background color. Yes, the image of the book adds some visual interest, but the text below the book is what, in my opinion, really sets the mood for the page. You can't help but fall in love with the site and book based solely on the type treatment. It's gorgeous: Clearly not a bad statement for a site promoting a design book.

FIGURE 1: http://forgeandsmith.com

FIGURE 2: http://shapeofdesignbook.com

http://evanrichards.co

http://tinybigstudio.com

Beautiful is better than ugly.

WordPress Themes

Studiofolio
A new versatile Portfolio and Blog Theme.

Demo

Buy

www.undsgn.com

WE LAUNCH IDEAS

Awkward is a small independent product design company. We build simple, useful products.

MORE ABOUT US

WE'RE BUILDING SHIPMENT

Share and review your design projects.

www.madeawkward.com

DESIGN STUDIO

ESTUDIO DE DISEÑO

Nuestros servicios abarcan un amplio rango de posibilidades en el campo del diseño desde branding e identidad corporativa hasta diseño editorial y diseño digital. Contamos con una gran experiencia en campos tan diversos como la moda o la producción de diccionarios y trabajamos de manera conjunta con nuestros clientes para crear soluciones sólidas, innovadoras y eficientes.

PUBLISHING HOUSE

CASA EDITORIAL

Estamos convencidos de que la época actual es la más emocionante para estar vinculados al mundo editorial. Desde los tiempos de Gutemberg no se presenciaba tanta emoción vinculada al libro. Somos especialistas en concebir y producir contenidos de gran impacto cultural y, como editores, esperamos compartir nuestra pasión por los libros.

WE ARE INDEPENDENT

SOMOS BIEN INDIES

www.reynaranjo.net

Evolve

- ARTISTIC, INC. -

PORTFOLIO

SERVICES

ABOUT   BLOG   CONTACT

WE PLAN, DESIGN, & BUILD,

REMARKABLE WEBSITES

PALATINE HILLS ESTATE WINERY

An award-winning, historically-rich, and exceptionally friendly winery.

www.evolveartistic.com

No-nonsense web design, graphic design, creative strategy & project management.

Work   About

Contact

BCGEU Microsite
cantaffordchildcare.ca

A responsive issue-based microsite & petition for the BC Government & Service Employees' Union.

http://isaacgc.com

http://figmenta.com

ANDREW LOHMAN

I am a web designer, focused on crafting great experiences, making everything I touch better, smarter and easier to use. I specialize in responsive front-end design, HTML/CSS and web typography. *I believe simple is beautiful.*

PROJECTS

Some work. Some play. Some work in progress. All designed and coded with love. Brought to you by Dribbble.

http://andrewlohman.com

WE'VE GOT SOMETHING
BIG TO SAY

WE SET OUT TO CHANGE THE WAY WE THINK ABOUT HEALTH—TO MAKE IT HUMAN AGAIN.

OUR ABILITY TO DO THAT HAS JUST BEEN MAGNIFIED BY **100X**. READY TO FIND OUT WHY?

WE'VE BEEN
ACQUIRED!

We are proud to say that we have been acquired by a company that not only leads in consumer products, but is *the* leading company in consumer health. They do hardware. They breathe design. They are FastCompany's **second most** innovative consumer tech company (beaten only by Apple—and we're coming for you, Apple). They are:

www.massivehealth.com

A Big Button Array

When it comes to building a menu on a mobile site, it seems that many designers build a vertical list of text links. Sometimes there is an icon affixed to the front of the link, but the pattern is pretty common. In this chapter, we will look at a range of sites that take a different approach. On these sites we find that they make use of an array of big buttons. Most often, they are in a grid two buttons wide and as tall as necessary. There are many things to love about this style, but one of the most significant is the usability. Navigate these sites on your mobile device and you likely appreciate it as well. The buttons are easier to touch than thin rows of links. I am constantly frustrated with sites using lists of links that are too small, but here the buttons lend themselves to more square-like shapes. This makes them easy targets for your fingertip.

The Harris Farm Markets website is a prime example **(FIGURE 1)**. Here, the home page contains six large buttons that link to key sections of the site. You will no doubt notice that they are large rectangular shapes that contain text and an image. The size makes them easy to touch and very user friendly. Also, the images add a layer of information to the buttons and add a lot of visual appeal to the page. A few of the photos aren't exactly topical, but I can forgive this, as they give the page a much-needed visual boost.

On another site with a similar solution we see a bit of a twist on the idea: Check out bomfim.ca **(FIGURE 2)**. Here, the large buttons are portfolio pieces, and they lack the descriptive text. All the same, they clearly depict what you will get when you click on them. More importantly, I appreciate this site's design, as the buttons feel distinct and different. The artist didn't follow the exact same formula for each one. This gives each a unique style and makes the site so much more interesting.

FIGURE 1: www.harrisfarm.com.au

FIGURE 2: www.bomfim.ca

www.progresso.com

http://passmob.net

www.designcrowd.com

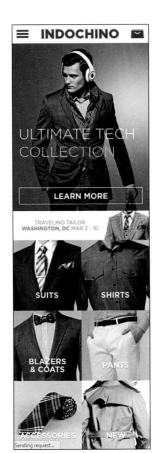

www.indochino.com Ⓜ

www.retailmenot.com Ⓜ

http://cibocalgary.com/menu Ⓜ

http://christinerode.com Ⓜ

www.1948london.com Ⓜ

www.morerare.com Ⓜ

www.diesel.com/m Ⓜ

Light on Dark

Before we dive into this topic I want to be sure to point out that the next chapter is the reverse of this one and showcases dark on light sites.

It might seem overly simplistic to differentiate between sites that are either light-on-dark or dark-on-light, but I think there is something to it as you consider the mobile environment. As you browse the collection of sites here in the light on dark section, I think you will recognize that there is a bit of a common feel to them. It is actually coincidence that so many of the sites here represent code-oriented products, whether it is a coding conference or a company focused on development. These sites have a dark feel to them that somehow resonates with the stereotypes of being a coder.

It is interesting to visit these sites on a mobile device; something I encourage you to do as I suspect that viewing them here in print won't have the same effect. A dark site like this on a mobile device forces the white text to pop. They have a very contrasting feel that is sharp and clean.

http://riothq.com

http://trins.ca

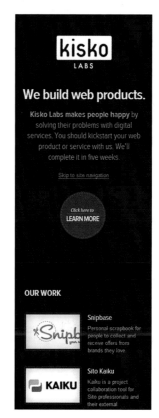

http://kiskolabs.com/#home

http://arrrrcamp.be

http://buildresponsively.com

http://blackwell.ca

http://badracket.com

http://getflywheel.com

www.formfett.net

http://thepixelbureau.com Ⓜ

http://yokedesign.com.au/about Ⓜ

www.tackmobile.com/products/start Ⓜ

Dark on Light

In total contrast to the last chapter, here I would like to feature a round of sites that have dark text on a light background. Most of the sites represented here create a rather stark contrast between the dark text and the light background. This nearly black and white feel gives the sites a crispness that is beautiful and easy to look at. On the flip side, if you compare this to the light on dark sites, I think you will find that those sites have more of a pop to them, while these feel far more subdued and contained. Less rebellious even. Bizarre as it seems to say, these sites just seem to feel more mainstream. It really is hard to believe that so much can be read into such a fundamental and seemingly stylistic design element as this.

A few of the samples here really serve as the pinnacles of this approach; Bread & Pepper **(FIGURE 1)** is a perfect example. Perhaps I am drawn to sites making use of beautiful ampersands, or more likely, I really feel drawn to the sharp contrast and easy-to-read style on these sites.

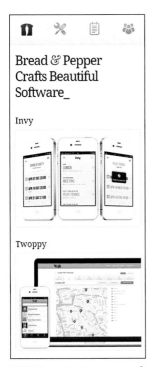

FIGURE 1: www.breadandpepper.com Ⓜ

http://urre.me Ⓜ

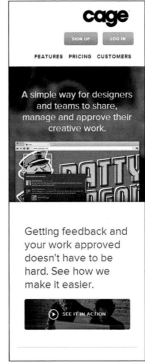

www.cageapp.com Ⓜ

http://envylabs.com Ⓜ

HOME   WORK   ABOUT   FEED

JOBS   CONTACT

A higher plain

http://builtbybuffalo.com Ⓜ

Ⓒ TV SAFETY   f 🐦 ✉ ⌄

SECURE YOUR TV TO PROTECT YOUR FAMILY

Our homes are a safe haven from the dangers of the outside world. Unfortunately, they also house a growing danger that we use every single day. Our TV.

Flat-panel TVs are tall, thin and can easily tip causing personal injury or death. Mounting your flat-panel to the wall is the safest option for securing your television. To highlight this solution and prevent further injury, TVsafety.org was created to educate the public on this growing danger and present safe solutions to protect families. It is our goal that together we can help to reduce TV-related injuries and create a safe environment for all to enjoy.

START EXPLORING BY CLICKING BELOW

www.tvsafety.org Ⓜ

hooray LABS

We **design** & **develop** ideas.

GRAPHIC DESIGN

We provide a range of perfectly fitted branding services, from a simple logotype to a full identity system.
We put the highest attention to details to make your brand memorable.

INTERFACE DESIGN

From first drafts to a carefully crafted user interface, we help you to find the right experience for your users by creating beautiful and intuitive applications.

WEB DEVELOPMENT

We use Ruby on Rails to deliver efficient, scalable and robust web applications. We

www.hooraylabs.com Ⓜ

Cart   Account

VS⬤   Store   Journal

VISUAL SUPPLY ⊚

VSCO   **KEYS**   FILM   CAM

VS⊚KEYS

VSCO KEYS™ IS A POWERFUL KEYBOARD SHORTCUT TOOL CREATED TO DRASTICALLY REDUCE IMAGE EDITING TIME IN ADOBE LIGHTROOM.

DOWNLOAD A TRIAL

WATCH VIDEO

LEARN MORE

http://visualsupply.co Ⓜ

http://typofonderie.com

http://smugandsauce.co.uk 🅜

http://zync.ca 🅜

http://bitfoundry.ca 🅜

Black and White

I didn't originally plan on having any sections on specific colors or color combinations in this book. However, as I researched the many hundreds and probably thousands of websites for this book, I was struck at just how many relied on a heavy use of black and white color palettes. Oftentimes, these were paired with an accent color, but still had a strong black and white base. It is actually really shocking just how prevalent this is. Showcased here is but a small sampling of the large quantity of options that could have filled these pages.

A gorgeous example of this is the Smug & Sauce agency website **(FIGURE 1)**. Here the black and white (and a bit of gray) color palette is pretty much used exclusively. The resulting tone for the site is rather powerful. It is not as though the site has some sort of massive visual punch; instead it comes off as more subtle, controlled, sophisticated and professional. I get the impression that this fits the agency well and helps the small shop convey their passion and commitment to their craft. I would also argue that the black and white palette allows their array of Shopify themes to really stand out. They look gorgeous and more appetizing on the crisp black and white design.

Another example I really like is the site for Life & Thyme **(FIGURE 2)**. Here the site sticks to the black and white theme extensively. Again, the resulting design has a powerful aesthetic that speaks volumes about the content of the site. One tiny detail I appreciate is the red ampersand in the logo. I pondered this element for quite some time, debating if it was good design or bad. I kept thinking it was bad because the one thing that is different on the page (colorwise) is the ampersand in the logo: a piece that seems rather insignificant. I have since come to believe that though the focal point seems unimportant, it is actually critical. The red gets your eyes on the logo for the site, and you can hardly resist reading it once your eyes settle on it. In a layout where everything is black and white, the small red pointer ensures you see the brand and name of the site, making it a powerful and critical component of the design. It is amazing how much power a simple dash of color can have when you exercise such extreme control in the rest of the design. As someone once told me, if you try to emphasize everything, you end up emphasizing nothing. This design directs the user's attention with the most subtle and simple of design elements.

FIGURE 1: http://smugandsauce.co.uk

FIGURE 2: http://lifeandthyme.com/who-we-are

http://mappeditions.com

www.jsnrynlds.com

INFORMATION

Belief is a New York City based skateshop & clothing boutique, as well as a lifestyle apparel brand. Our aim is to enroll our community into a positive and productive lifestyle. Heavily influenced by the NY hustle, we believe that you can achieve anything you set your mind to. To us, the term "Ever Upward" is more than just the NY state motto. It sums up our belief that if you strive to do what you love, you can reach your full potential in the face of any adversity.

VISIT

29-20B 23rd Ave
Astoria, NY 11105

DIRECTIONS

Google Map
Hopstop Directions

CONTACT

(718) 721-4444
info@beliefnyc.com

HOURS

Mon - Sat: 11-8
Sunday: 11-6

http://beliefnyc.com/info

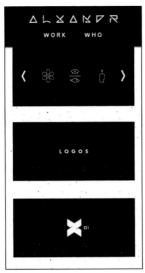

www.alxandr.us Ⓜ

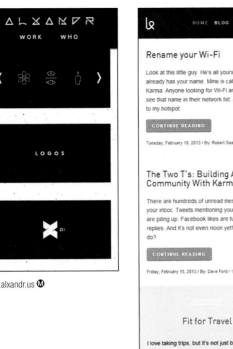

Rename your Wi-Fi

Look at this little guy. He's all yours. In fact, he already has your name. Mine is called Robert's Karma. Anyone looking for Wi-Fi around me can see that name in their network list, and connect to my hotspot.

CONTINUE READING

Tuesday, February 19, 2013 / By: Robert Gaal / 1 Comment

The Two T's: Building A Community With Karma

There are hundreds of unread messages in your inbox. Tweets mentioning your company are piling up. Facebook likes are turning in to replies. And it's not even noon yet! What do you do?

CONTINUE READING

Friday, February 15, 2013 / By: Dave Ford / 1 Comment

Fit for Travel

I love taking trips, but it's not just because of the places I go to or the people I meet. It's not just about the pictures I take, or the souvenirs I buy. What I like most about travel is optimization. It forces you to only have things with you that are brutally necessary for you to complete your journey. What kind of shirts can I do without?

http://blog.yourkarma.com Ⓜ

Hi. I'm Aaron – a designer with a penchant for plenty more, currently living in Brooklyn, NY.

READ MORE

Metro Magazine
CONCEPT, UX & VISUAL DESIGN, FRONT-END DEVELOPMENT

Voltage
CONCEPT, UX & VISUAL DESIGN, FRONT-END & WORDPRESS DEVELOPMENT

Crazy Blind Date
CONCEPT, UX & VISUAL DESIGN

Principle Six
CONCEPT, UX & VISUAL DESIGN

http://aaron.mn Ⓜ

09. Toward a New Education

Low Cost, Scalable, Distributed & Above All: Personalized

Dec 29, 2011

I spend a lot of time thinking about the future, trying to figure out where the next big wave of change is going to hit. I lived through my first in the 80s, with the personal computing revolution. That gave way to others in the 90s & oughts: webs 1 and 2.0. Here in the tweens we have a new wave sweeping the globe: the smartphone and tablet computing revolution. So, what's next?

www.strangenative.com

I team originality with nifty design to craft a brand identity worth a thousand words. After all, less is more so simplicity is king here at Larkef. Each design comes with a free warm, fuzzy feeling.

What I do

Jord by name, icon lover by nature. I'm fanatical over detail and function, hence my love of the nuts

http://larkef.com

hangloose

sito in fase di ristrutturazione nel frattempo potete:

★ leggere il nostro manifesto

⬇ sfogliare il nostro book

↻ visitare il nostro vecchio sito

★ giocare con il nostro albero di natale

studio hangloose srl
p.iva 04320381009

viale del poggio fiorito 27
00144 rome
ITALY

tel [+39] 06 542 28 511
fax [+39] 06 542 20 720
info@studiohangloose.it

Company certified by CERMET for:
quality control ISO 9001:2008
information system security ISO/IEC 27001:2006

www.studiohangloose.it/en

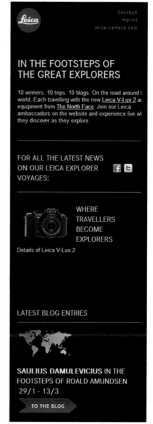

Deutsch
Imprint
leica-camera.com

IN THE FOOTSTEPS OF THE GREAT EXPLORERS

10 winners. 10 trips. 10 blogs. On the road around t world. Each travelling with the new Leica V-Lux 2 a equipment from The North Face. Join our Leica ambassadors on the website and experience live wi they discover as they explore.

FOR ALL THE LATEST NEWS ON OUR LEICA EXPLORER VOYAGES:

WHERE TRAVELLERS BECOME EXPLORERS

Details of Leica V-Lux 2

LATEST BLOG ENTRIES

SAULIUS DAMULEVICIUS IN THE FOOTSTEPS OF ROALD AMUNDSEN 29/1 - 13/3

TO THE BLOG

http://leica-explorer.com

06

Design Elements

In my books, design *elements* are different from design *styles* in a rather simple way. Styles represent overall design approaches or visual tendencies. On the other hand, elements are but small pieces used in a design or in the structure of a site. While most of the elements here are common in everything from desktop to phone sites, there are a few that are mostly found only on phone-based interfaces. It is these elements I want to consider and examine how they impact mobile designs.

As it turns out, this actually becomes a section that could easily appear in my main Idea Book series. Though there are some special situations relating to mobile devices, the results are actually rather universal. This is exciting, as it demonstrates just how far the mobile world has come.

Navicons

Though I am uncertain where navicons originated, or even who came up with the goofy name, their saturation into the mobile space is off the charts. I could practically fill an entire book with sites using navicons. So what is a navicon? They are those little buttons with three horizontal lines. When clicked or tapped, they expand into a menu in some way. Some slide in menus from the side, some are drop downs and others simply expand into a section of the content of the page. The result is that the navicon connects users to navigation that is tucked away. They are extremely handy for hiding navigation systems from view until they are needed and are a fantastic way of streamlining an interface.

I actually learned an interesting and important lesson about this little gem of an element. I was helping my wife build and launch a website for her new business. A part of this included a mobile interface for her site. I made use of a navicon and tucked the navigation inside it. She took one look at it and expressed that she had never seen such a thing before and had no idea what to do with it. I was a bit dumbfounded, as I was in the final stages of writing this very book. Navicons were on my brain, and it never occurred to me that people might not know what to do with them!

The point is that we always have to be cautious of the knowledge and experience we carry with us. Ordinary people that don't browse thousands of mobile websites to write a book don't have the same level of exposure as I do. And you, the reader, are likely to have far more knowledge and understanding of mobile websites then the average Joe. I learned such a powerful lesson from this simple experience that I couldn't resist including this anecdote to challenge you to carefully consider the expert knowledge you carry into your work.

In all of the examples here I have provided two views. One before the navigation is activated and a second after it has been selected. Though you clearly cannot see how it transitions, you can still see how it interacts with the other content on the page. You will notice that in a large portion of the samples, the navicon is joined by the word *menu*. Given my experience with my wife, this makes a lot more sense. Perhaps someday it won't be necessary, but for now it can be a point of confusion for users and it is reasonable to consider if the audience for your site needs extra help finding the menu.

http://jure-stern.si

http://byassociationonly.com

www.netokracija.com

http://useaconcept.com

www.spangen.dk

www.northbounddesign.com

http://plainmade.com/company

Slide-Out Sidebar Menu

One interesting approach to navigation that I found quite often was a slide-out sidebar menu. Oftentimes this was activated by a navicon (see previous section). I believe this approach originated with Facebook, and has been adapted to countless other sites. It turns out that having the menu slide in and take over the screen is a rather clear way to demonstrate to the user that they have activated a menu. It actually ends up feeling like the designer magically created a new space in the layout. It's an ingenious approach that I think we will see more and more.

In the examples here, I provide before and after views, demonstrating what the design looks like without the menu exposed, and then of course what it looks like with it expanded. Case in point is the website for Speakers' Spotlight **(FIGURE 1)**. Here you can see how the menu overlaps the page but leaves a bit of the site revealed. This is actually an interesting strategy. Some sites completely cover the content, while others take this approach: I think they both have their merits. I like this approach if only because it lets the user see they haven't changed pages, but only activated a menu system. They can still see the page they were on and that things haven't changed. It simply helps the user understand where they are and what is happening. Eliminating confusion is a remarkably important aspect of mobile design and development. In my experience, confusion is one of the fastest ways to get me to abandon a site, especially a mobile one. In fact, on mobile sites my tendency to dump a site seems much greater, and my sensitivity to confusion far greater. And I am a web person: Imagine the average user!

In several of the samples here you will notice that the designers have packed more into these pop-out menus than they might have in plain old navigation links. You will find in several of them search forms, and in others image-based navigation like thumbnails. This is perhaps the real beauty of this technique: You can tuck away more extensive navigation systems that would otherwise clutter up a site. In fact, I think this approach offers the opportunity to create more visual navigation systems than a design could otherwise accommodate.

One assumption most of the samples here make is that users will know to click again on the navicon to hide the menu. One sample, however, provides a much more clear method to allow users to exit the navigation: a very simple X. If you look at the Osborn Barr website **(FIGURE 2),** you will see the expanded menu. The simple X is easily understood and is pretty universal. As I have previously highlighted, cutting through the confusion of an interface is critical, and this is a remarkably simple way to do just that.

FIGURE 1: www.speakers.ca

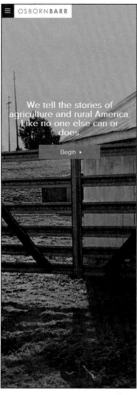

FIGURE 2: http://osborn-barr.com

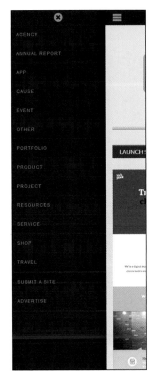

http://fltdsgn.com/kick-point

www.nixon.com

http://thisisthebrigade.com

www.youneedabudget.com

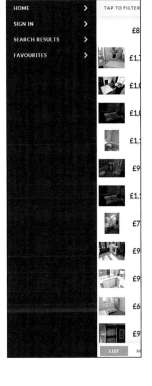

http://kangaroom.co.uk Ⓜ

www.thehaberdashfox.com Ⓜ

Forms

As I mentioned in the Responsive Forms chapter, forms can be a bear to deal with. For this reason, I wanted to include an additional batch of sites demonstrating strong examples of mobile forms. Simplicity and clarity are fundamental in making sure your forms don't discourage people from completing them. One of the finest examples collected here is the contact form found on Paravel's website **(FIGURE 1)**. Note how clear the form is. Each field has a large easy-to-read label. Required fields are clearly marked with a vivid red asterisk. On this site, you will notice the lack of a theme or other quirky design for the form. Historically many sites made use of crafty form designs that reflect their typical function: translating the contents of the form into an email that is sent to a site administrator. This sort of thematic approach becomes unnecessary on the mobile web and simple, clear forms like this are vastly preferable, as they are much easier to use.

You will no doubt notice that every example provided here features forms in a single column layout. And in most cases, the form fields and buttons span the full width of the page. Another approach many sites use is that the labels for the fields are included in the field itself. When the user clicks on or taps the field to enter data, the placeholder text and label disappears. The only potential downside to this is that a user may forget what they were entering into the field. This approach is good for condensing things, but it does run the risk of confusing users.

Of the examples I have provided here, one of them stands out as rather unique: Take a look at the contact form on Simple's website **(FIGURE 2)**. This form is nothing like the others, and is actually very much like the crafty ones I described as out of place. And while I stick to that assessment, I will say that there is almost always a situation where such a universal statement doesn't apply. In this case, the form is extremely simple and therefore has the potential to work in such a design.

I encourage you to approach the design of your web forms with caution but with an open mind. In many cases, you want to stick to a safe streamlined approach, but always be on the lookout for unique ways to set your design apart.

FIGURE 1: http://paravelinc.com/contact.php

Request an Invitation

Dear Simple,

My name is _____ and my email address is _____. Please let me know when Simple is ready for me.

Request Invite

FIGURE 2: www.simple.com Ⓜ

SAY HELLO

First Name

Last Name

Company

Title

Email

Phone Number:

555

555

5555

Message

Submit

http://mogreet.com/contact Ⓜ

Contact

If you are requesting a quote, please refer to the FAQs first.

Name:

Phone Number:

Email Address:

What is 2 + 3

Message:

Please send as much info as you can. This will help me give you a quote accurately.

Submit

www.cibgraphics.com/contact Ⓜ

http://m.jlern.com

http://global.tommy.com

https://yourkarma.com/contact

www.yielddesign.co

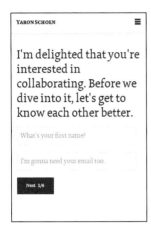

YARON SCHOEN ☰

I'm delighted that you're interested in collaborating. Before we dive into it, let's get to know each other better.

What's your first name?

I'm gonna need your email too.

Next 1/6

http://yaronschoen.com/project-inquiry

What can we do for you?

Do you have a project you'd like us to work on with you? Do you have an RFP for us?

Your name *(required)*

First | Last

Email address *(required)*

Company

How would you like us to contact you?
◉ Email ○ Phone ○ Skype

Tell us what you need. *(required)*

Do you have a Request for Proposal (RFP) document, or a brief?
○ Yes ◉ No

I would like to add more project info...

Send enquiry

www.markboultondesign.com

MailChimp [Log in]

Get Started with a Free Account

Sign up in 30 seconds. No credit card required.

Email

What's your email address?

Username

Password

Create My Account

By clicking this button, you agree to MailChimp's Anti-spam Policy & Terms of Use.

© 2001-2013 All Rights Reserved. MailChimp® is a registered trademark of The Rocket Science Group.

https://login.mailchimp.com/signup

We'd love to hear about your project. Together, let's set things in motion.

YOUR NAME*

Name

COMPANY*

Your Company, Inc

E-MAIL*

you@your-email.com

CONTACT #*

XXX-XXX-XX-XX

MESSAGE*

Submit

http://wearemovingthings.com

Icons

Icons are an element of web design that is rather universal. We can find icons at work in nearly every website these days. We see them most commonly as simple social media icons, and beyond that in informative and decorative ways. Icons are so common, in fact, that I have featured them in every volume to date of my Idea Book series. Amazingly, there are still things to discover about these useful elements and how designers have put them to work.

One example that actually sparked the creation of this category is the Zync website **(FIGURE 1)**. On this site, in the upper right corner is an icon that matches the Google Maps app icon. It is used to link to the location of the company on Google Maps. With icons, designers typically like to closely match them to a website via custom designs and colors. In this case, the designer simply leveraged an existing icon that many people are familiar with. This is an extremely effective approach that clearly demonstrates the power icons carry. They can instantly communicate with users and you instinctively know that this icon will get you a map to their office. Zero confusion and zero explanation needed.

Another website that uses icons prominently that I found particularly interesting was the website for Elliot Condon **(FIGURE 2)**. While icons as pointers to social media are nothing new, this designer's use of them is rather distinct. One icon caught my eye as a misfit here: the ACF one. As it turns out, it links to a web property operated by the individual. As a whole the icon set looks great, but I can't help wonder if the ACF link is somewhat lost there. Functionality aside, the icons and their decoration become a critical visual element in the design of the site.

While icons can play a supportive role, they can also be critical to the core message of a site. A perfect example of this is the wishlistme.com site **(FIGURE 3)**. Here, the three large icons aren't just pretty, they clearly articulate the purpose of the site. The first two are not new icons, but are well known. The designer cleverly leverages the common knowledge people will have of these icons. The final one is extremely literal and is easy to understand in the context of the site.

One place we frequently find icons is in navigation systems. Such is the case on the Standbuy site **(FIGURE 4)** where the icons are woven into the navigation of each profile page. As you frequently find, the icons are based on common patterns. As it turns out, icons are not an area where people tend to innovate; instead we find that most designers leverage them for the meaning they carry based on users' previous experience.

FIGURE 1: http://zync.ca Ⓜ

FIGURE 2: www.elliotcondon.com Ⓜ

FIGURE 3: http://wishlistme.com Ⓜ

FIGURE 4: www.standbuy.us Ⓜ

www.pyramidlabs.in

www.polarbearapp.com

www.breezejs.com

http://unionpgh.com

http://byassociationonly.com/about

www.digitalatelier.ro/#/services

www.wearegrand.com

http://lorenzoverzini.com

Circles

If I were to say that one design element presented in this book surprised me, it would certainly be this one. This chapter, in fact, is a perfect example of how the book takes form. As I comb through the entries, elements and styles start to stick out, and the prevalent use of circles quickly became apparent. This approach is fairly visible in the full desktop world: In fact, I have a full chapter on circles in design in Volume 3 of my Idea Book series. So perhaps I shouldn't be surprised by the style appearing on the mobile web. I suppose it is just because on such small screens, it seems strange to rely on circles instead of larger squares or rectangles. And yet, I am sure that as you browse the samples here, you will find they are remarkable examples that leave a distinct impression on you.

The About Our Work site **(FIGURE 1)** is a rather vivid example of this. Here, the circles aren't necessary; the images could easily have been made without them. And yet, I really love that the circles partially containing the elements give them a common ground. And the way the images break out of the circles gives them an interesting dynamic that draws the eye. What a strange and interesting way to steer the user's focus. It makes me wish they had stuffed a call to action into one. And finally, the simple use of decorative circles in the background unifies the design and yet avoids an annoying polka-dot look.

Another rather interesting example with a very distinct style is the personal site of Matt Imling **(FIGURE 2)**. Here the attention-grabbing power of the circles is used to create a series of eye-catching elements that communicate the core ideas of the site. You quickly find out who the site is about and what he does. And I have to admit, for a mobile site, it has an extremely distinct look and feel even though it relies on such simple elements. Perhaps I have mistakenly underestimated the power of such a simple shape.

Perhaps my favorite sample here is the MoreHazards.com site **(FIGURE 3)**. Though CDs might feel rather unnecessary these days, the visual of one is still an indicator of music. On this site, the use of circles to create the look of a CD clearly communicate the purpose of the site. The use of circles becomes literal and echoes a physical factor of the site subject matter.

FIGURE 1: www.aboutourwork.com Ⓜ

FIGURE 2: http://mattimling.com Ⓜ

FIGURE 3: http://morehazards.com Ⓜ

http://siyelo.com Ⓜ

https://status.heroku.com

www.samgoddard.co.uk

http://applecrumbs.com

http://awesomenyc.com

http://zoltangarami.com Ⓜ

http://gosillk.com Ⓜ

http://supermamarazzi.com Ⓜ

www.themealings.com.au Ⓜ

Illustrated

Illustration is an age-old design element that is at home in any time period and can be combined with nearly any design style. I have yet to find a style that doesn't work well with illustrations. And though this is a powerful statement, I actually have a different reason for loving illustration as a web design element. Simply put, it makes a design unique. Illustrations are tied to the styles and abilities of the artist that created them. As a result, they are inevitably distinct. Granted, if you work from stock illustrations, you may not be the only one to use the artwork. Or, if you work in a common style, you run the risk of blending in. Even still, illustrations, unlike nearly any other design element, can single-handedly give your site a distinct and memorable flavor.

A perfect demonstration of this is the Front End Design Conference website **(FIGURE 1)**. The illustrations on the site, as well as those used to construct the layout, help the site stand out from the many other conference sites it has to compete with. In such a situation, it is extremely unlikely that a competitor will pick up on the same style and theme. The result is a distinct brand and experience that you are more likely to remember.

In other cases, the use of illustration is far less dramatic and serves more of an informational and support role. Such is the case on the Treehouse website **(FIGURE 2)** and the Colbow Design site **(FIGURE 3)**. On these sites, it is tempting to say that the illustrations fill a hole that a photograph could; however, I think there is much more at work here. Notice how the styles of the sites and the color palettes so closely connect with the illustrations. This, I believe, is yet another powerful aspect of illustrations: They can be carefully woven into the style of your site and add a powerful level of continuity to your design.

One of the samples here that I really love is the Javier Y Marta site **(FIGURE 4)**. On this site we find a small amount of illustration combined with some decorative elements and a very decorative typeface. The result is that the illustration feels woven into the fabric of the site. Everything about the design has a distinct illustrated style and stands out.

And perhaps one of the most exciting things about this approach—as far as mobile goes—is that it so strongly contradicts the very clean and minimal styles ruling the web right now. These sites feel even more distinct, memorable and fun to browse as compared to so many of the stripped-down mobile sites we often get.

FIGURE 1: http://2012.fromthefront.it

FIGURE 2: http://teamtreehouse.com Ⓜ

FIGURE 3: www.colbowdesign.com Ⓜ

FIGURE 4: http://ladisparatadaboda.com Ⓜ

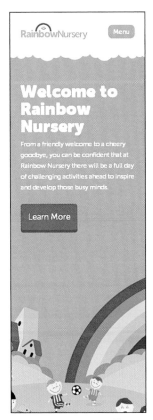

Welcome to Rainbow Nursery

From a friendly welcome to a cheery goodbye, you can be confident that at Rainbow Nursery there will be a full day of challenging activities ahead to inspire and develop those busy minds.

Learn More

http://myrainbownursery.co.uk

Webdagene 2012

26.—28. september, Oslo Kongressenter

Vs.

Norges viktigste webkonferanse:

3 dager. 30 foredragsholdere. Ekspertene møtes til duell. Webdagene gir deg ammunisjon for å lykkes på web.

Se video fra konferansen, bildene på Flickr og blogginnlegg fra Webdagene.

Josh Clark
Josh avslører seiglivede myter om mobil og beskriver kunsten å designe fremtidsvennlige løsninger.

Jeremy Keith
Media queries er ikke nok – effektiv responsiv design må

http://webdagene.no

http://gingerwhale.com

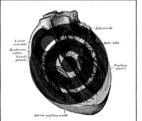

This is a Visual Metaphor

Whether it's a **logo**, a **website**, an **application** or a **user experience**, I believe design is about getting to the heart, uncovering the essence and expressing it with elegance and simplicity.

'Work.
I work in a wide range of design disciplines including identity and print, but my main focus is in web and UX design.

Identity Design
Half Pint Chef
Half Pint Chef is a cookware and kitchen e-commerce website that caters to kids.

http://joshuaturner.com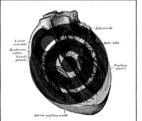

http://lensco.be

www.doubledcupcakes.com Ⓜ

http://americanmadetattoo.com/mobile
Ⓜ

www.applove.se Ⓜ

Texture

In the majority of sites presented here, texture is used as a decorative background element. One popular approach right now is to use a textured background and a rather sparse foreground. The design primarily relies on the structure and beauty of the content and less on extra design flourishes to create the experience. This removal of structural decoration makes the designs vastly easier to apply in a responsive world. A textured background that everything can slide around on is naturally appealing. I think, however, that even though this is the case in the samples here, there is often more to it than such a simple view of the style. Let's review a few of the sites to get a better idea of what I mean.

First up is Dusty Cartridge **(FIGURE 1)**. This site makes use of a fabric-style textured background, which happens to be an extremely popular approach right now. It's subtle, and adds a lot of richness to the design. Here the style meshes well with the main logo and branding of the site and provides a nice support design flourish to the page. In this case, the style is a nice step away from the glossy tech world and the site has a nice, organic feel to it.

As much as I have talked about texture in web design over the years, it always amazes me when I see an approach that feels unique and new. Such is the case on the Travel Oregon website **(FIGURE 2)** where we find texture woven into the overall style of the site and not just relegated to a supporting background role. Sure, there is a subtle background texture on this one, but look past that and there is so much more. I am truly inspired by the minimalist illustration that is somehow oozing with texture. It perfectly captures the essence of a state so well known for its natural settings. Even more amazing to me is the typeface chosen for this site. The font used here in the main links somehow manages to have a subdued and subtle hint of texture. The result is that it feels more natural and less forced. All too often, texturized sites feel overdone, but this site has none of that. The overall style so perfectly fits the site's topic that I can't help but love it.

Wii U Console Review

19 hours ago by Chad D'cruze

Whether you were a fan of it or not, you cannot deny that the original Wii simply went gangbusters back in 2006. Now we finally we have the Wii's successor – the Wii U. Armed with yet another unique controller and a vision to win back the hardcore gamer, can Nintendo restore faith in its lost audience? But more

FIGURE 1: http://dustycartridge.com

Oregon isn't a place you see as much as you do. You can sight-see our beautiful coast, volcanic mountains, crystal-clear lakes and deserts that stretch as far as the eye can see. If you're looking for world-class pinots, some of the best food and craft beer in the country, epic cycling, kayaking, windsurfing or just about anything else-ing, look no further.

Better yet, don't look, come out here and leap.

Activities, Events & Attractions

SO MUCH TO SEE & DO

In Oregon, there's always something to do. You can play world-class golf, cycle along hundreds of miles of designated bike lanes, take road-trips to wine country, hunt for fossils or get lost in the moment of a brilliantly crafted scene of play at

FIGURE 2: http://traveloregon.com

www.oxideinteractive.com.au

FIGURE 3:

www.enochs.co.uk

CouchDB

About ▾

Apache CouchDB™ is a database that uses **JSON** for documents, **JavaScript** for **MapReduce** queries, and regular **HTTP** for an **API**

DOWNLOAD
Version 1.2

ℹ️ A Database for the Web

CouchDB is a database that completely embraces the web. Store your data with JSON documents. Access your documents with your web browser, via HTTP. Query, combine, and transform your documents with JavaScript. CouchDB works well with modern web and mobile apps. You can

http://couchdb.apache.org

ABOUT
SHIRTS
CONTACT

APPAREL FOR RESPONSIVE-BUILDING, MEDIA-QUERYING WEB CITIZENS.

YOU DECIDE

SIZE US UP AND VOTE — WTH

SHOW ME THE SHIRTS →

375 VOTES

FRIENDS DON'T LET FRIENDS FIX WIDTHS.

CURRENT LEADER:

FRIENDS HELPING FRIENDS

A true friend would never let a friend put themselves in danger. Promote a healthy CSS lifestyle in your school, workplace, or developer meetup with our fixed-width friendship t-shirt. Keep this

http://dressresponsively.com

---

nuances minérales

luminosité · durabilité · écologie

luminosité

Nos systèmes de peintures minérales sont écologiques et dotés d'un très bon écobilan.

Sans dérivés de pétrole, nos peintures sont l'héritage de traditions anciennes mais s'adaptent admirablement bien aux besoins les plus modernes.

Fortement conseillé en intérieur, notamment pour les écoles et hôpitaux. Leur grande qualité et durabilité font des produits KEIM la marque la plus vendue en peinture minérale depuis 1878.

Contactez-nous pour plus d'information sur nos produits non polluants, respectueux de l'environnement et à caractère durable, pour des conseils,

www.nuancesminerales.ch

BAHSTON FILM CRITIC

Reviews   Commentaries   Cahntact Me

Latest Posts   📶

Eastwood's RNC Speach and Directorial Honesty

Monday September 3rd, 2012

A lot of people have given Clint Eastwood grief for the manner in which he delivered his message at the RNC this past week. Count me in the minority of those who thought his delivery was just fine but that take issue with the substance of his message. As a film fan it goes without saying that I admire and respect Eastwood for his work on screen and behind the camera. ...More ➤

The Dark Knight Rises

★★★★

Monday August 6th, 2012

Have you ever tried to build a house of cards? With each successive story the house becomes less and less stable. That is sort of the way I feel about sequels - especially since Hollywood feels obligated to

http://bahstonfilmcritic.com

CLEARMENU

TEXMEX

SPORTS BAR

FINE DINING

Why are restaurant website menus so terrible? Too often they exist as dysfunctional blights on otherwise very nice websites (though surely many are nicer than others). Some of us at Unit Interactive thought it would be nice to show a few examples of how these vital pages can quite easily be done better. What follows are our fun exercises in usable menus.

http://clearmenu.unitinteractive.com Ⓜ

home   salon   massage   body   skincare   makeup
nails   staff   packages   gift cards   products
schedule

berkshire
salondayspa

hair
facials
waxing
massage
body
nails
makeup

need to schedule an appointment?

Ready to relax and indulge yourself at Berkshire Salon and Day Spa? Schedule an appointment today to take advantage of featured services such as facials, waxing, hair, manicures, pedicures, and dermatology.

www.berkshiresalondayspa.com Ⓜ

PAMPA
FURNITURE

STORE LOCATIONS

THE PAMPA STORY

DECOR & STAGING

CONTACT US

◆ avweb designs

www.pampafurniture.net/mobile Ⓜ

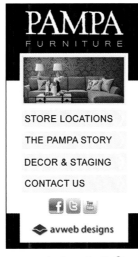

VOLTA
HOME AUTOMATION

Home

What is home automation?

What can I automate?

Why Volta?

Contact

HOME AUTOMATION MADE AFFORDABLE

Enjoy high-tech gadgets at a low-tech price with Volta Home Automation.

Volta Home Automation simplifies your home and your life. It puts you in control of your electronics, climate controls, security system, lighting, and more. Turn lights on and off, change the music, lower the thermostat, or activate the security system—all from your comfy couch or halfway around the world.

With home automation, you have the most control and the most freedom all in one service. Life just got a whole lot easier!

Learn more

**BUILD THE IDEAL
AUTOMATION SETUP FOR
YOUR HOUSE**

http://voltaautomation.com Ⓜ

Transparency

I originally started this category with a single example, thinking it would be rather easy to fill. Since CSS3 now allows one to so easily create transparent containers, it seems that they have become rather commonplace. On the desktop this might be true, but it could not be further from the truth on the mobile web. In most of the samples I explored where transparency was at work on the desktop site, it almost always disappeared on mobile ones. Things would shift and slide around, and the transparency would most often become unnecessary. As a result, it took a fair amount of effort to find the examples presented here. In each book a topic or two becomes a challenge: This was the unexpected challenge for this particular book.

On the Chevy website **(FIGURE 1),** I found what is perhaps the most practical use of transparency I have seen. Most often transparency is used for decorative purposes, but as you can see in this screen shot, here it is rather functional. Many mobile sites have menus that expand when touched. A common problem I encounter when navigating such sites is that it is hard to tell where the menu starts and ends. As you can see in this example, when you expand the menu the rest of the page is grayed out, much as you would get with a typical lightbox effect. This shows the user what has just appeared and where they should focus their attention. After browsing many hundreds of sites, I found this refreshing and it stuck with me as one of the key learning points of my research. The mobile web can be confusing, especially when something is added to or removed from a page: anything you can do to make it abundantly clear to the user is a good thing. It is a rather simple nuance that provides significant benefits.

In other situations like the United Pixelworkers website **(FIGURE 2)** or the Evomail example **(FIGURE 3)**, the use of transparency is purely aesthetic. In these cases, the transparency works to beautify the page and is not a critical component of the design. It adds style, but doesn't serve some grand strategy. While we can often find profound meaning in the most mundane of details, we should never forget that sometimes things are just pretty to look at.

FIGURE 1: www.chevrolet.com/corvette-sports-cars.html 🅜

FIGURE 2: www.pixelivery.com 🅜

FIGURE 3: http://evomail.io 🅜

http://coworkchicago.com 🅜

http://jonwhitestudio.com

https://sweetbasilvail.com

http://madamegautier.co.uk

www.typeform.com

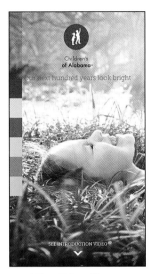

www.childrens2012.org

Our focus is less on providing an extensive database of teas, and more on focusing our attention on the new & exciting teas that capture the season. That's because we believe the real magic behind tea comes from your experience, not just your taste buds.

http://steepmonkey.com

http://supereightstudio.com

http://www.kitchenprague.com/en

Jumbo Photographs

A current popular style in web design is the use of large photographs as design elements. We often find them at work as background images, with content placed over the top of them. Now let's observe how this element has been adapted to the mobile web. Most of the examples here are responsive sites, and I am simply showing the phone-based version of the site's design. While a large image could slow a site down, the overall simplicity and streamlined nature of these sites makes them efficient layouts. And on the mobile web, where minimalism reigns king, these layouts feel refreshing and unique.

The results of a site based on a large image can be beautiful, and the site of Christina Fischer **(FIGURE 1)** is a clear demonstration of this. It isn't hard to love the way the photograph is woven into the page. The dark road in the foreground serves as a lovely contrast to the white text on top of it. Interestingly, the photograph naturally leads you up to the navigation.

In other situations, the photograph is far less decoration and actually a part of the site's content. Lindalino **(FIGURE 2)** is a clear demonstration of this. Here the photographs are the content, and the images are boldly worked into the site and its design. Instead of content contained inside the site, the images become the site.

The Mine website **(FIGURE 3)** demonstrates another common approach you may be familiar with. Countless websites set up to sell a mobile app—such as this one—make use of this simple approach. The amount of information packed into the image is priceless in terms of rapidly telling a user what they are looking at. One look and you immediately know the site is all about an iPhone application.

One thing is for sure—when using a large image like this, it has tremendous power to set the mood of a site. For example, compare the following sites: journal.everest.com **(FIGURE 4)**, theafterbedtimesessions.com **(FIGURE 5)** and magisto.com **(FIGURE 6)**. All three have large photographs as backgrounds. Each also has a totally distinct tone and mood. The images are core to setting the stage for these sites. It's an amazingly effective and simple approach.

FIGURE 1: http://christinaf.ch

FIGURE 2: www.lindalino.com

FIGURE 3: http://getmine.com

Choose your hard

Waking up at 6.30am to exercise is hard. Waking up at 8am seems easy, by comparison.

Resisting the temptation to eat sweets is

Waiting for journa...

FIGURE 4: http://journal.everest.com

http://getbarley.com

http://partlyblue.com Ⓜ

http://teamkernel.com/#main-nav Ⓜ

www.teamnine.ch Ⓜ

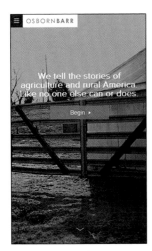

www.osbornbarr.com

www.bluestepstudio.it

www.adidasretailjobs.com

www.julianabicycles.com

Blurred Background Images

In photography, it is commonplace to use blurred backgrounds, or bokeh, to focus the viewer's attention on the subject matter of the photo. In particular, you will find this approach at work in portrait photography. The strategy is easily adapted and applied to the web. And of course many people have done exactly that: Let's dissect a few samples to see how this technique can be used on the web.

Start by taking a look at the Mookie x Sweetyams site **(FIGURE 1)**. On the mobile interface, the blurred background image is like a mash of greens and is impossible to make out. If you view it on a desktop, you will be able to tell that it is a forest view because you can see more of the image. Given the limited view of the image on mobile devices the image becomes decorative and not informative. The greens give the page punch and style and allow the solid whites to pop out. The results are absolutely gorgeous. And the blurred background does its job perfectly by creating contrast for the content and adding beauty.

In other cases, such as Launch This Year **(FIGURE 2)**,the blurred background is completely lacking in content and simply appears to be a blur of colors. We have no idea what it is—and it doesn't matter. Again, the results are the same: The blurred background creates depth and directs attention to the elements that *are* in focus.

While many examples of this approach might use radically blurred-out backgrounds to beautify a page, some sites like Fitsby **(FIGURE 3)** use a less blurred image. Here, the image is actually important to the communication of the page. It is blurred out to help the text pop, but if you focus on the background, it is easy to see the content of the image and to learn about the app the site is selling. Clearly, it has something to do with working out and doing something at the gym. It sets the context for the usage of the app and gives the page a dose of visual style.

FIGURE 1: http://mookieyams.com

FIGURE 2: http://launchthisyear.com

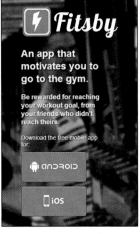

FIGURE 3: http://fitsby.com

www.everpix.com/landing.html

http://handsome.is Ⓜ

http://madewithover.com Ⓜ

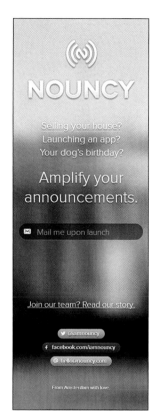

www.nouncy.com Ⓜ

http://nicolasmarx.fr/ Ⓜ

http://thisisdallas.github.com/Simple-Grid

http://charitablethemes.com

http://joemck.ie

www.tapfit.co

07

Site Types

In my Idea Book series, I always have a large section where I highlight a variety of different types of sites, based on their purpose or industry. It is always an important part that adds real value to the book. As I considered and planned this section, I began to realize that—with a focus on addressing the needs of mobile sites—it is a potential gold mine of ideas. When it comes to mobile, it is often very hard to compare how common problems are solved. The following collections of sites each focus on a single topic and you can therefore compare solutions easily.

If you're designing a mobile site and don't happen to be dealing with one of the subject areas listed here, please don't disregard this section. All sites have common components, and I am certain that you can identify elements of various sites here that fit your needs. Look at the details and how each site addresses problems in its own unique way.

Portfolios

Portfolio sites are consistently one of the most common types of sites I receive when I begin accepting entries for my books. As such, this section is always easy to fill with a rich variety of samples. This mobile-focused book is no exception.

Two sites here take a very similar approach, manufauque.com **(FIGURE 1)** and pauljohns.com **(FIGURE 2)**. In both of these you see a very similar format, though clearly the style applied to the structure is radically different. If you break these designs down to their most basic elements you will see that they are built on bands of content. Each row, or band, changes layout as the screen size changes. This allows each row to remain in its order, while adjusting to fit the screen. In the end, this is an easier approach than a more complex layout based on interconnected parts. Both of these designs also have very minimal decoration, further adding to the ease of adapting the design.

Another common thread here is the prominence of the work. None of the samples here force you to go beyond the home page to see the individual's work. Bringing samples to the surface in this way has been a trend for some time, but I think the need to address mobile users has further forced the issue. If you consider a mobile user looking at your portfolio, it seems to make good sense to get your work on the front page. Desktop users have a short attention span that feels long when compared to that of the average mobile user. As such, getting to the point rather quickly is extremely important. While this approach is effective in quickly showing users your work, it does come at a price. Packing this many images into a single page can radically impact the load time of the page on mobile devices. As such it is important to consider your approach and balance the initial impact with the burden it carries.

One note: All of these samples—and many other portfolio sites—are missing clear calls to action. If you're building a portfolio site you clearly have a goal. Are you trying to get work? If so, put a prominent element into your design that compels your visitors to take a step toward hiring you. When you focus on such a goal, it becomes a guiding principle for your site.

FIGURE 1: http://manufauque.com/portfolio

FIGURE 2: http://pauljohns.com

http://jag.is

www.colazionedamichy.it

http://brunobernardino.com

http://jeremypeters.co.uk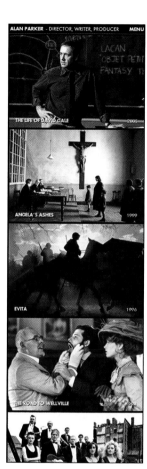

http://alanparker.com/film

www.mthoogvliet.nl

PORTFOLIO
JOURNAL
RESPECT
CONTACT

LUCK IS
PROBABILITY TAKEN PERSONALLY

FILE .012
INTEL

Designer-developer Stephen Caver has been interested in the inner workings of the web since he was a kid. His attention to detail is evident in his site designs, which emphasize clean displays of content while facilitating great user experience. Stephen has experience in information architecture, interaction design, HTML and CSS. He has worked with clients such as the World Wide Web Consortium, Change.org and the Mozilla Creative Collective.

When he's not designing beautiful websites, Stephen can be found passionately following the Los Angeles Dodgers, killing things on Xbox, and spending time watching history and science-based reality shows.

- TWITTER
- DRIBBBLE
- FLICKR
- GOWALLA
- TUMBLR
- FACEBOOK
- LAST.FM
- YOUTUBE
- AMAZON

http://stephencaver.com Ⓜ

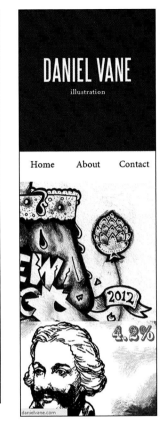

DANIEL VANE
illustration

Home   About   Contact

2012

4.2%

danielvane.com

http://danielvane.com Ⓜ

Bryan Connor

WORK
BLOG
SAY HI

Small desk, big ideas.

I work with great people to make better products.

Designing great experiences for users.

I make applications, tools and communities that care about the people using them. A few product ideas of my own creation are currently in the works. I value collaboration, big ideas, and relationships with great people.

Visualizing meaningful data.

I see data visualization as one of the toughest challenges a designer can tackle. The visualizations I make communicate meaningful data to a broader audience. I write about other's visualizations that deserve your attention on The Why Axis.

http://bryanconnor.com Ⓜ

M

Select ▾

WEB DESIGN &
ILLUSTRATION

HELLO

My name is Matt Hamm. I'm a illustrator & web designer

I am the Creative Director & co-founder of Supereight Studio Ltd. alongside Pete Orme.

I'm extremely passionate about the web, design, illustration, animation, typography, web standards, user experience & photography. I've got tons of experience designing logos, icons & mascots & producing unique online brand experiences.

MORE ABOUT ME

www.matthamm.com Ⓜ

Personal Landing Pages

The personal landing page is very similar to a type of site that I covered in Volume 2 of my Idea Book series: the business card site. These micro sites serve as a sort of virtual business card, and personal landing pages take a very similar approach. The only potential difference is that these tend to be mini link portals to the individual's profiles and pages on other networks, like Twitter, Facebook, Behance, blogs, etc. They also serve as a contact point that enables visitors to connect with and contact the individual. This may be via social networks, but also includes basics like e-mail and phone.

As usual, let's focus on a few individual sites, starting with Pat Dryburgh's mini landing page **(FIGURE 1)**. Interestingly, he doesn't give his name, what he does, or anything more than an illustrated headshot and a few links. While it might seem easy to criticize this on first take as clearly lacking in information, we don't know his intentions for the site. I would speculate that the site is not a source of revenue for him. If anything, it reminds us to consider how we invest our time: I am pretty sure if he needed a fancier personal presence, he would have it. This mindset is something I think we seldom embrace. We get all caught up in what we are *supposed* to have and we forget to step back and think about what we really need. As designers, this is one of the most powerful ways to come up with creative solutions. I am excited that I can showcase such a radical range of sites in one book, as I sincerely find this one inspiring.

In another nice example, Michael Dick **(FIGURE 2)** has a slightly different approach. His mini site is a mini portfolio. Given that much of his work is online, a simple list of links to his creations serves as a powerful portfolio. Anyone that doesn't have time to get a portfolio online should take a look at this. If your portfolio is web work, jump-starting your online presence with such a simple approach is a solid idea that can likely be completed in relatively short time. I also appreciate that the individual's face is attached to the site. The only change I would be tempted to propose is to include his name more clearly. Regardless, it does a great job at providing a simple landing page for the individual.

FIGURE 1: http://patdryburgh.com Ⓜ

FIGURE 2: http://m1k3.net Ⓜ

http://benjaminminnich.com Ⓜ

http://garrettwinder.com Ⓜ

www.manifakture.com

http://ampersandrew.com Ⓜ

www.lukebott.com Ⓜ

http://yaronschoen.com/table-of-contents Ⓜ

http://john.do

http://dooid.me/karalundquist

http://andrevski.com.au

http://jonphillips.ca

Agencies

Agency sites are a very close tangent to the standard portfolio site. However, given the needs of an agency, we tend to find noticeably different approaches. One element that really stands out to me is the prominence of a concise sales pitch. Sometimes we find this element on portfolio sites, but it seems to be rather universal on agency sites. For example, the Web Development Group **(FIGURE 1)** site proclaims that they "evolve brands & keep it cool." Statements like this sum up a company and often reveal some element of their culture. If you consider the responsive nature of these sites, you will notice that most often these sales pitch statements retain their prominence and are a critical part of communicating with visitors.

It is amazing how much in common such a disparate set of samples can have. Note, for example, how almost every sample here has some sort of content rotator on its homepage. Granted, content rotators probably appear on at least 90% of all sites created these days (note my whimsical statistic creation). Though I may not have the hard numbers, it is clear that rotators are insanely popular. That said, it is very interesting to observe how these sites work such an element into a mobile environment.

Another interesting aspect that seems to set these sites apart from the basic portfolio site is the thematic nature these have. While there is still a common use of minimalism here, you will notice that these sites weave very distinct styles and thematic elements throughout their designs. For example the Zookeeper website **(FIGURE 2)** has very distinct style to it that creates a memorable experience, though it doesn't beat you over the head with some kitschy approach. I know the word *thematic* tends to draw up much more topical design styles, but I think the term applies in this case.

FIGURE 1: www.webdevelopmentgroup.com

FIGURE 2: http://Zookeeper.com

www.yellowpencil.com

http://webcoursesagency.com

www.room150.com

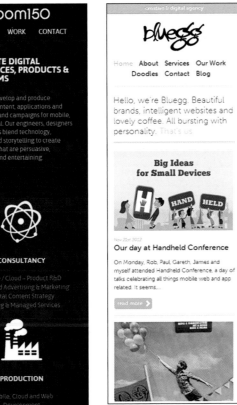

www.bluegg.co.uk

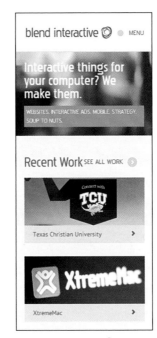

www.blendinteractive.com

www.gummyindustries.com

http://cubicleninjas.com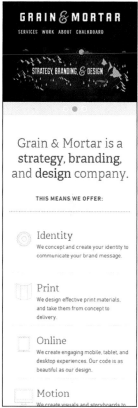

www.tilde.io

http://studiomds.co

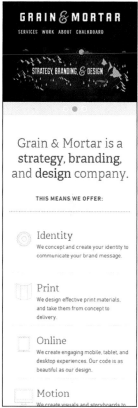

http://grainandmortar.com

Mobile App Sites

A chapter on mobile websites that sell mobile apps in a book about mobile design—it doesn't get much more meta than that. Yeah, it might feel a bit obvious. But the point at which mobile websites and mobile apps meet is a very important one. The mobile app industry is growing like crazy and is easily justified in being represented here. In fact, they demonstrate something few mobile sites can—a clear conversion point that sells the product and gets it in your hands immediately.

One aspect of these sites that is not all that surprising is that most of them show the product through screenshots. These screenshots clearly show the intended context for the product. This is actually really helpful when considering if the app is intended for a smartphone or a tablet. For example, contrast the Wee Rockets **(FIGURE 1)** and Static **(FIGURE 2)** websites. It may seem predictable, formulaic or like taking the easy way out, but this approach is actually really practical. The information it communicates is critical.

Another critical component is the conversion point that drives visitors to the finish line to make the purchase. Interestingly, such a button is very prominent on many of the sites here. For example, the enormous button on the Wally's Bac Attack **(FIGURE 3)**. In contrast, Breaks **(FIGURE 4)** has the link at the very bottom of the screen. It requires the user to scroll through a lot of content before getting to it. It is tempting to say this is wrong, but it is really interesting to consider that the user must first get the sales pitch. They have to scroll through all the content describing the product. This begs the question: Are you better off getting the button in front of the user straight away, or is it better to give the sales pitch, and then drive people to convert? It seems to me that the second option makes more sense. I imagine fewer people push the magical App Store button, but I bet the conversion rate is higher. Just a guess, but I feel extremely comfortable making it. This leads to the realization that A/B testing is what you really need to do, and this can include some radical variations like button placement. Hopefully, the samples here provide much-needed inspiration for trying new design variations.

FIGURE 1: http://weerockets.com Ⓜ

FIGURE 2: http://static.freshbyt.es Ⓜ

FIGURE 3: www.wallysbacattack.
co.uk Ⓜ

FIGURE 4: http://breaksapp.com Ⓜ

www.read-thai.com

http://overgram.co Ⓜ

http://bakkenbaeck.no Ⓜ

http://madewithover.com Ⓜ

http://savethegold.com

Making wishes come true.

Never receive the wrong gift again.
Share your wishes and say thanks.

Available on the
App Store

Toast on Facebook   Toast on Twitter

Like 317   Tweet 40

Blog   Jobs   Privacy   Terms of Service   Help
(@toasthelp)
Giveatoast GmbH © 2012

http://toa.st

~Who's on your?~
RADDDAR

What is it

Raddddar is a web based app where you can
easily see and connect with people around you.
It's a service based on coincidence and location.
Just a simple opportunity, to meet people near
you.

Alpha Release

Login with Facebook

Login with Twitter

Login with Google

Get updates

✔ No feed.

✔ No followers.

✔ No walls.

✔ No personal details.

✔ Free.

Tweet 27   Like 58   / Twitter /
Facebook /   © / V&G Contact

www.radddar.com

≈   HOTLST

"Let me add you to my
hotlst…"

The easiest way to prioritize your prospects,
recruits, and clients. Know who to target and in
what order, from hottest to coldest. Your *hotlst*.

Available on the
App Store

Soon to be available on BlackBerry OS 10 and
Tablet OS as well.

http://hotlst.co

With its delightfully clever way to set time, Rise is one of the simplest alarm clocks you will ever use.

www.simplebots.co

https://heml.is

Weathertron is a new kind of weather report: an instant, accurate data visualization of your entire day. Now you can *see exactly* what the day has in store — minute by minute. Available for iPhone®, iPod Touch® & iPad®.

http://theweathertron.com

http://duocode.co/apps/payme

Product Sites

The mobile sites presented here represent a range of products, though most of them ended up being food-oriented. There are a few other products in the mix though, including one piece of online software. I always love an odd mix of sites that still fit in a category for some reason: It always produces some interesting insights. For example, it is rather clear that physically showing your product is one of the most prominent goals of these sites. Each sample here has the product front and center in a way that allows it to appear on the first screen of content.

One interesting commonality between these sites is that, for the most part, they are informative sites, not intended to enable you to make a purchase on the spot. That said, it is interesting to see what their most important action item is. And at times, sorting out the site's primary call to action isn't always so simple.

Some sites like Illy Issimo **(FIGURE 1)**, Klondike **(FIGURE 2)** and Skinny Cow **(FIGURE 3)** all have clear points of action. "Find Illy Issimo," "Find one" and "Get the skinny"—these calls to action clearly attempt to direct the user to a desired outcome. And obviously, these are all steps toward purchasing the actual product, though the purchase isn't to be made online.

In contrast, consider something like the Mountain Dew mobile site **(FIGURE 4)**: Here the desired outcome is not apparent. The site seems more geared toward connecting with visitors, and in some way feels almost like a check in the box—"Yup, we have a mobile site, check." And to be frank, sites for products have often been something I scratched my head about. Brands want them, and at times they can be helpful, but honestly, when is the last time you visited a site to learn more about some random product? It seems inevitably hard to actually pin down why the site exists. Ironically, the more successful the brand, the more pointless it feels. I don't need a site to tell me about Mountain Dew—I don't need the site to help me find the product. Why then would I visit the site? And this, of course, is a huge challenge to face. This question makes the samples here all the more compelling. Because, chances are, you're working on a type of site that serves a very clear purpose. Look at how those that struggle for a purpose handle it, and I think you will find some refreshing ideas. And don't get me wrong: These sites are great examples of their niche and are, on their own, great examples of mobile web design and development.

FIGURE 1: http://us.illyissimo.com Ⓜ

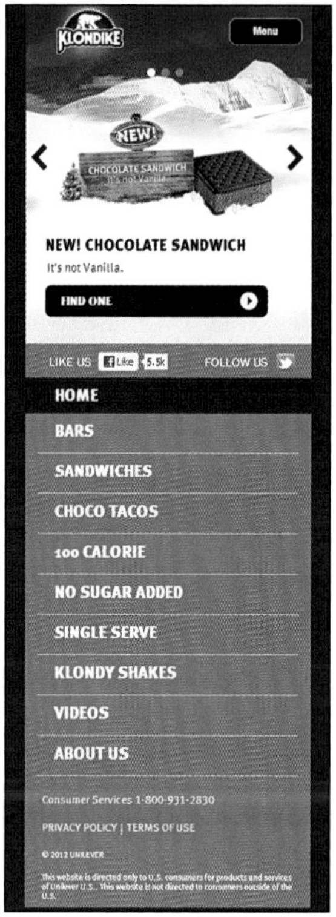

FIGURE 2: http://m.klondikebar.com Ⓜ

FIGURE 3: http://www.skinnycow. com Ⓜ

FIGURE 4: http://mountaindew.com Ⓜ

www.getdonedone.com

http://kershaw.kaiusaltd.com

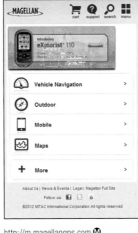

http://m.magellangps.com

http://m.hersheys.com/reeses.aspx

http://m.hersheys.com/icebreakers/
frost-products.aspx

http://m.fancyfeast.com

m.brancottestate.com

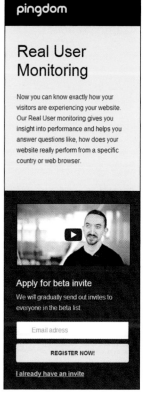

www.pingdom.com/rum

Mobile E-Commerce Sites

As always, I love a diverse collection, and I think you're really going to see that in action here. This chapter on mobile e-commerce sites includes everything from small start up T-shirt shops to full-blown mega-retail online stores. And, as always, I worked hard to avoid the obvious sites that we all know very well already (*cough* Amazon). The fundamental purpose of the sites is the same: to sell stuff and ship it. But it is abundantly clear that the problems these sites face are very different. The small shops have few products, and may have agile teams that can move rapidly. In contrast, the big retailers have thousands of items, legacy systems to deal with and probably more non-technical issues than you ever want to see. As a result, it makes this collection even more diverse and fun to consider.

For example, I kind of love that the Belong website **(FIGURE 1)** makes you work through their mission statement before ever seeing a product. And given the size and style of the type, it is kind of hard not to read it. The result is that you form a connection to the brand. It is also clear that this isn't some mega brand with marketing people trying to "connect" with you. Instead it feels authentic, engaging and inspires me to *want* to buy something. It is really hard to imagine a more powerful sales approach. In contrast, we can look at the Five Simple Steps site **(FIGURE 2)**, which also happens to be a reasonably small operation. Here you see that their goal is to get the product in front of you. There is no sales pitch, no catchy intro or mood-setting photos. Nope, you simply get the product with titles, photos and a clear buy button.

Another site that vividly demonstrates different needs and approaches is the MacDonald Hotels & Resorts site **(FIGURE 3)**. In this case, they are selling an experience, and not as much a tangible product. As a result, the elegant feel of the site, the beautiful photography and the clear sales points are critical to setting the mood and closing the deal. Booking a hotel always feels like a bit of a gamble, so there is no reason to plant doubt in your visitors' minds. Another point of inspiration for a site like this is the checkout process. It is much more complex to book a room than it is to buy a T-shirt. As such, they had to more carefully craft the flow of the site on mobile devices.

FIGURE 1: http://wearyoubelong.com

FIGURE 2: www.fivesimplesteps.com

FIGURE 3: www.macdonaldhotels. co.uk

www.shultzilla.com

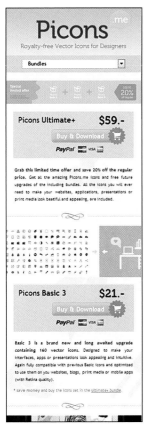

http://picons.me 🅜

http://m.junkyard.se 🅜

www.wormsigntshirts.co.uk 🅜

www.eastworksleather.com 🅜

http://m.rei.com ⓜ

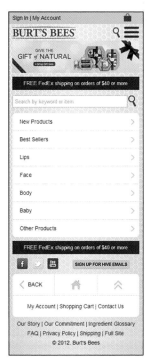

http://m.burtsbees.com ⓜ

http://vsco.co/store ⓜ

http://shop.tylerfinck.com ⓜ

http://skinnyties.com Ⓜ

http://fitforaframe.com Ⓜ

http://us.suitsupply.com Ⓜ

www.tsovet.com Ⓜ

News Sites

To be rather blunt, the news industry isn't exactly a part of the web I frequently look to for inspiration—especially in the area of design. That said, the industry as a whole isn't totally lost. In fact, if you're at all in tune to the world of responsive web design, you are likely familiar with the Boston Globe site **(FIGURE 1)**. This site has received so much attention that I considered leaving it out, due to the amount of exposure it has already received. But I thought it was important to include, as it represents a major milestone in the web community at large.

The problems that news sites face are epic, and they are perhaps the most daunting type of site one might build. That said, these problems make them some of the most exciting to see done well. What hurdles might they face? Well consider the following: They have a continuous flow of new content that is contributed by a great number of people. The sites feature massive amounts of content, sections and other types of subsections. They require advertising. The first issue has to be epic in terms of getting people to contribute their work and format it in a consistent way. I can't imagine the effort it must take to make sure each and every article is set up in a consistent way. That said, designing a site like this for one screen size seems hard: Designing it so it will adapt to any screen size in a meaningful way seems impossible. Again, this is why I find these sites inspiring.

Beyond the Boston Globe, there are several other news outlets that have very well-done mobile and responsive sites. Among those featured here we find the Houston Chronicle **(FIGURE 2)** and Time **(FIGURE 3)**. These sites serve as a gold mine of ideas for how to lay out content-dense sites, many of which can easily be adapted and used on many different devices.

On the other end of the spectrum, we have some news channels here that are web native. Most notorious among these might be Mashable **(FIGURE 4)**. Not so surprisingly, the site feels very different from a traditional news organization. Here, we also find a more prominent use of social media than in any of the other examples I have provided. The idea of using social metrics to drive interest to content is far from new, but the fact that is still so prominent and in use demonstrates that the approach still has merit and value.

At the end of the day, these sites address issues that some of us may never have to deal with. Even still, we can find nuggets and ideas from them to inspire our own projects.

The Boston Globe

DECEMBER 13, 2012

SECTIONS   MY SAVED   Q

Latest news

Another juror dismissed in Moore trial

For the second time in a week, a juror has been dismissed in the murder trial of Dwayne Moore, forcing the jury to restart deliberations again. 9:06 am

Boehner says Obama risking fiscal cliff stalemate

In remarks to reporters, House Speaker John Boehner said President Obama has not been serious about cutting spending. 10 minutes ago

Russia, NATO chief say Assad losing control

Syria's most powerful ally and the secretary general of NATO said separately that Syrian rebels are getting closer to winning the country's civil war. 9:05 am

Four to leave Patrick's cabinet

Suffolk County Sheriff Andrea Cabral will join the Patrick administration as the state's public safety secretary.

FIGURE 1: www.bostonglobe.com

HOUSTON ★ CHRONICLE

DECEMBER 13, 2012

SECTIONS ▾   Q

Gerald Harbert, AP AP2010

Kin of those killed in Gulf disaster slam BP settlement

By Harry R. Weber
10:39 AM

Relatives of some of the 11 men killed in the 2010 Gulf of Mexico rig explosion want a federal judge to reject British oil giant BP's multibillion-dollar settlement of criminal charges stemming from the disaster.

⤷ **Tougher offshore scrutiny? Not yet**

LATEST

'Lincoln' leads Golden Globes with 7 nominations
11:28 AM

FIGURE 2: www.houstonchronicle.com

TIME

Follow   Apps

SECTIONS ▸   Q

◄ ► Man Shoots Himself Inside Ala. Federa...

CHIP SOMODEVILLA / GETTY IMAGES

The Fed Ties Interest Rates to Jobs: A Very Big Deal

BY CHRISTOPHER MATTHEWS

- The Fed's Big Unemployment Move
- Is The Housing Recovery Just an Illusion Created by the Federal Reserve?
- 📷 The Recession in Pictures: America Copes with a Stagnant Economy

Egypt Divided: The Brotherhood Fails to Find Common Ground

Poll Results: Readers' Choice for Person of the Year

A Dream Abandoned: Last Man on the Moon, 40 Years Later

Don't Eat Daddy's Cookies: How to Talk Pot with Your Kids

Report: Nurse in Kate Middleton Prank Hanged Self

feedback

FIGURE 3: www.time.com/time

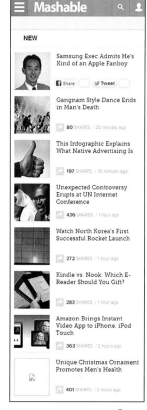

☰ **Mashable**   Q   👤

NEW

Samsung Exec Admits He's Kind of an Apple Fanboy

Share   Tweet

Gangnam Style Dance Ends in Man's Death

80 SHARES / 20 minutes ago

This Infographic Explains What Native Advertising Is

197 SHARES / 35 minutes ago

Unexpected Controversy Erupts at UN Internet Conference

436 SHARES / 1 hour ago

Watch North Korea's First Successful Rocket Launch

272 SHARES / 1 hour ago

Kindle vs. Nook: Which E-Reader Should You Gift?

283 SHARES / 1 hour ago

Amazon Brings Instant Video App to iPhone, iPod Touch

363 SHARES / 2 hours ago

Unique Christmas Ornament Promotes Men's Health

401 SHARES / 2 hours ago

FIGURE 4: http://mashable.com

07

NEWS SITES

Mercedes Ml pagata con due assegni da 20mila euro di una ditta chiusa da anni

Compravendita d'auto, arrestato lo specialista nelle truffe

💬 (0) |

TREVISO – Questa volta, dopo svariate denunce a piede libero per truffa legate alla compravendita di auto, è stato pizzicato in flagrante e tratto in arresto.

PRIMA PAGINA ▾
Treviso
Castelfranco
Conegliano
Mogliano
Montebelluna
Oderzo Motta
Valdobbiadene Pieve di Soligo
Vittorio Veneto

www.oggitreviso.it

VIA E-MAIL · **Evening·Edition** · LOCALE ▾

Good news readers! Use the toggle above to select the edition you want to read every day. More editions coming soon.

Tuesday, December 11, 2012

GAY MARRIAGE DRAFT LEGISLATION TO OFFER CONCESSIONS FOR OPPOSING RELIGIOUS GROUPS

U.K. Culture Maria Miller began her campaign to introduce same-sex marriages in the country by telling Parliament that religious groups will not be obliged to conduct ceremonies against their wishes, a reassurance sought by her fellow Conservative MPs. She also said she would protect these groups with a "quadruple legal lock". The first part will be a declaration on the cover of the legislation that no church will be forced to marry same-sex couples, the second will be an amendment to the Equality Act to stop discrimination lawsuits against churches, the third a guarantee that European law will not be allowed to interfere internally and finally a provision that will ban the Church of England and its counterpart in Wales from offering same-sex marriages altogether. Miller faced intense questioning from MPs after her statement, including one Tory MP who asked her if she also proposed to introduce other forms of marriage such as polygamy.

NELSON MANDELA SUFFERING FROM LUNG INFECTION

Former South African President Nelson Mandela, who has been hospitalised since Saturday, is suffering from a recurrence of an unspecified lung infection. "Doctors have concluded the tests and these have revealed the infection, for which Madiba is receiving

http://evening-edition.com

Hanukkah Lights in the Big Sky

MINNPOS

SECTIONS ▾ | Search 🔍

Weather Support Us   Log In or Register

THE GLEAN

Strib opens talks to sell off stadium land

BY BRIAN LAMBERT | 05:38 AM

Electronic pull-tabs get attention; Iron Range wants to lure filmmakers; EPA delays air rules; woman takes file-sharing case to Supreme Court; "Nutcracker" to use canned music; and more.

Read Tuesday PM Edition

More ›

Flood of casino money brings challenges — and opportunities — for reservation schools

BY STEVE DATE | 08:19 AM

For some kids, the lure of "18 Money" makes it difficult to focus on school. But some tribes are making educational gains.

www.minnpost.com

---

theguardian   Top stories ▾   ≡

🕐 48 min ago

Life expectancy around world shows dramatic rise, study finds

Men are living 11 years longer and women 12 years compared with 40 years ago, although health problems are also rising

🕐 5 hours ago

Government pays Libyan dissident's family £2.2m over MI6-aided rendition

Sami al-Saadi, wife and four children were secretly flown from Hong Kong to Tripoli where he was tortured by Gaddafi police

🕐 5 hours ago

Maria Miller faces parliamentary investigation into her expenses

Standards watchdog to open inquiry into culture secretary's second home arrangements after claims in Daily Telegraph

http://m.guardian.co.uk

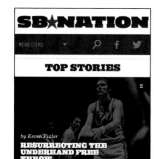

SB★NATION

MENU ITEMS

TOP STORIES

by Kevin Fixler

RESURRECTING THE UNDERHAND FREE THROW

NBA

Metta World drops the 'Peace'

by Seth Pollack, Dec 13, 11:27a

Just when you think you've heard the last from Metta World Peace, he does a 15-minute Skype interview shirtless from his bed in which he talks about the progression of his music career and how that relates to his name changing ways.

THE HOOK

Amazing defensive gains fuel Warriors

by Tom Ziller, Dec 13, 11:01a

The Warriors' offense is playing just about as well as it did last year. But the defense has gone from among the worst in the league to average ... without Andrew Bogut. How?

COLLEGE BASKETBALL

Big East finished?

by Rodger Sherman, Dec 13, 8:55a

The Big East might collapse Thursday,

www.sbnation.com

≡ **TNW** ▼ Q

Top Stories from Across The Next Web

BY **MATTHEW PANZARINO** — 13 DEC '12

US court rules Apple's iPhone infringes on three patents held by Sony and Nokia owned MobileMedia

A US court has ruled that Apple's iPhone infringes on three patents held by MobileMedia Ideas, a shell company that exists to enforce patents held by Nokia and Sony. reports... Keep reading →

BY **ANNA HEIM** — 13 DEC 2012

Google offers free Wi-Fi Internet connection in 150 Brazilian bars for 90

http://thenextweb.com

View the open letter

A **SWEARY** ANGRY YET **ACCURATE** COMPARISON OF POLICY

Labor ■ VS. LNP

CREATED BY A HUMAN BEING WHO DOESN'T BELONG TO ANY POLITICAL PARTY BUT DOES GIVE A SHIT

👍 Like 403,906 people like this. Be the first of your friends.

SUPER FUCKING AWESOME NBN

SHITTY, SLOW HALF-MEASURE THAT WILL NEED TO BE FIXED LATER

Window size: 413 x 1080
Viewport size: 397 x 967

http://dontbeafuckingidiot.com/

 the ONION
America's Finest News Source
☰

Chuck Klosterman Corners Guy At Party Wearing Dio Shirt

Goldman Sachs Announces They're Blowing Up A Nursing Home And There's Nothing Anyone Can Do About It

Nate Silver Vows To Teach Chris Berman How To Read

Narrow Gaps In Bathroom Stall Doors To Be Widened Monday

Employee Offering Suggestion At Meeting Slowly Grows Quieter And Quieter Until Eventually Squeaking 'I Don't Know'

www.theonion.com

Universities

Let's face it, when you think of industries on the cutting edge of web design and development, universities are not the first places that come to mind. In fact, I believe the presumption with many people would be that this is an industry so slow to respond that they will not show progress in the area of mobile and responsive design for a long time. Shocking as it may be, this is a radically inaccurate assumption.

I worked in a university for many years and I am all too familiar with how slow things can move and how hard it can be to push for progress. With this in mind, the samples here are even more impressive. The designers navigated the barriers and pushed out awesome mobile designs. Even more impressive is that so many of these are the main home pages, which are perhaps some of the most difficult to get consensus on. My hat goes off to those behind these projects.

If we are to learn but one lesson from these sites, it would be how they handle intense content needs. Universities tend to have an insane amount of online content, from admissions information to all of the material for each department, program and course. The amount of content is staggering. I was intrigued as I studied the ways these sites handled the home page.

Some sites will take the approach you find on the Temple University site **(FIGURE 1)**. Here, the lists of links are replicated in various styles on the main page. The different blocks seem to be grouped in somewhat logical ways, but it is a lot to absorb. Other sites, like the Harvard site **(FIGURE 2)** take a very different approach. Here we find that they have attempted to predict what users will want: In particular, you will notice that the content is geared toward existing students and not prospects. We cannot say if this is good or bad, but only hope that they studied the site's traffic to realize that mobile traffic was primarily existing students and not potential ones. I actually think this makes good sense. And, of course, it is clear to see that they created a layout that resonates with what mobile users are familiar with. The best part of this, in my opinion, is that it creates large squarish buttons as opposed to narrow rows of buttons.

Another approach that I appreciate is that found on the University of Michigan website **(FIGURE 3)** Here we find yet another list of links, but with one nice change: They are grouped. The list of ten links is broken down into three categories. This makes it so much easier to locate relevant information. It is interesting that much like the Harvard site, the focus is on existing students. But potential students are not totally left out, as they have a few links at the very bottom. This seems like a really nice balance. The Grand Canyon University site **(FIGURE 4)** is also a nice mobile example, but imagine how much slicker it would be with a few groupings to break down the links.

FIGURE 1: www.tuj.ac.jp Ⓜ

FIGURE 2: http://m.harvard.edu Ⓜ

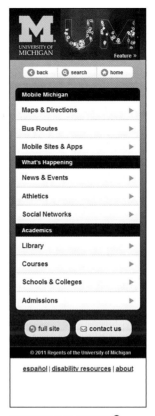

FIGURE 3: http://m.umich.edu Ⓜ

FIGURE 4: http://m.gcu.edu Ⓜ

www.wm.edu

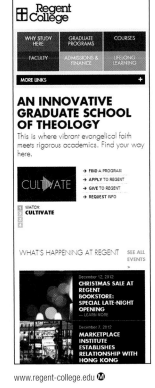

www.regent-college.edu

www.lancs.ac.uk

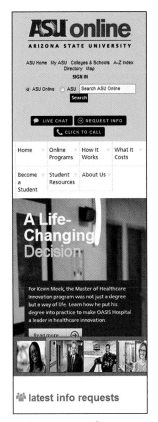

http://asuonline.asu.edu

http://m.ncsu.edu

http://m.uiowa.edu/home

http://stories.cstudies.ubc.ca

https://m.rit.edu/home

www.mobap.edu

http://arts.stanford.edu

www.cambria.ac.uk

www.luiss.edu

Government and Politics

Our instinct might be to presume that government and political sites might be behind the times and total disasters. The reality is actually quite the opposite. This is a niche of sites that has some very forward-looking samples. And if you think about it, it isn't all that surprising. Politics are big business, and they have the funds to invest in solid websites built on best practices.

Perhaps the most noticeable pattern among these sites is the focus on news. All but a few of these sites prominently feature this section. It is probably tempting to place donation links front and center. But you will notice most of the sites reduce this action item to a simple link. Understanding what people want from your site is incredibly important and should be the focus of the site. I think sometimes business owners get lost in what they want from the site and forget the users in the process.

One aspect of these sites that is likely to be easy to overlook is the color palette. Though all but one of the samples here are U.S.-based government sites, you don't find that the standard red, white and blue color palette is beat to death. Though it is at work, it is usually woven into the style of the site in a much more restrained fashion. At times, resisting the urge to overdo it with a cliché can be hard: These sites clearly demonstrate that avoiding such a crutch can be really powerful. For example, I really love the way the Obama/Biden site **(FIGURE 1)** makes use of a primarily blue and light gray palette. In particular, the variety in these colors seems perfect: instead of sticking with a single blue, they make use of a range of blues. The result is beautiful.

Another approach that I think is really spot on relates to the way forms are used in these sites. In the two samples with prominent forms, you may notice that they are very much styled to suit a mobile user. They are large and easy to click on. And once the task is completed, the text is also large and easy to read. Frankly, I feel that mobile forms are most often difficult to use. These large, bold samples demonstrate how easy a form can be and are great samples to draw inspiration from.

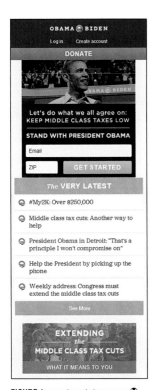

FIGURE 1: www.barackobama.com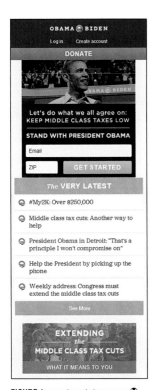

www.mittromney.com

www.gop.com

www.democrats.org

Discovering Mildenhall's Canberra

PHOTOGRAPHS FROM THE BIRTH OF OUR CAPITAL

• • • • ○

Housed in one of Australia's most-loved buildings, the Museum of Australian Democracy at Old Parliament House brings the journey of Australian democracy to life—presenting its past, present and possible futures.

Enjoy a range of innovative exhibitions, tours and public programs that challenge and inspire. There are also special activities and spaces for children to explore.

Admission and opening hours

http://moadoph.gov.au

www.hannity.com

Zachary Chesser: A Case Study in Online Islamist Radicalization

The Homeland Security and Governmental Affairs Committee issued a staff report February 20, 2012, detailing the internet radicalization of a homegrown terrorist to violent Islamist extremism and the inadequacy of U.S. policy to counter online radicalization.

The report presents a classic case study of how quickly online radicalization can occur compared to the traditional

www.hsgac.senate.gov

http://aids.gov

www.ri.gov

m.ksdk.com Ⓜ

http://apps.usa.gov Ⓜ

www.socialmediapoliticians.com Ⓜ

Blogs

Blogs have become a fundamental part of how the web works, and optimizing these experiences for mobile users is a necessary step. Collected here is a sampling of different approaches. Naturally, we can find a variety of ideas to inspire our own designs. Let's look closer at a few of the samples to see how they have optimized their content for mobile users.

On Tom Lloyd's website **(FIGURE 1)**, we find one of my favorite approaches. The style of the blog layout is extremely clean. It relies on solid colors and has a clear hierarchy in the content. The result is a blog that is super easy to scan and read. I think this highlights a key element of mobile blog design, and mobile design in general. We must always consider how it will be to *use* the interfaces we design. Often we may try to get overly clever and lose sight of the goals. On a mobile blog, we just want people to read the content. As such, a design like this one is perfect for ensuring users can easily consume the content.

Another great example is the blog of David Jones **(FIGURE 2)**. The design of this site is based on a much richer visual. Instead of a minimal approach, the design is more stylized. Fortunately, the content and hierarchy of the page is still clear and easy to read. The result is a design that reflects its creator's personal style, while maintaining a high degree of usability. As I have so often said in this book, maintaining this balance is a key to successful mobile web design.

Codrops **(FIGURE 3)** is one of my favorite blogs. The ideas I would like to propose here are actually closely related to this. When you know a site, you have a predetermined set of expectations. Often you have a visual memory that helps you quickly identify the site. I think it is important to understand the most important elements of your design and make an effort to weave these into your mobile site. The Codrops site successfully does this. Its distinctly styled headlines are core to the visual identity of the site, so the mobile site also features a distinctive blue header with white logo. Fortunately, all of these elements made their way into the mobile interface. I know that personally, I am tempted to really strip a site down for the mobile experience. We should approach this process with caution, carefully assessing what elements are critical for maintaining a common brand experience across all devices.

Tom A Lloyd
One of them designer types

LOVEFiLM. Hate Email.

20th November 2012

As some of you might know, my Bluegg buddy Rob has had a number of issues with how LOVEFiLM communicate when it comes to tone of voice and content. Yesterday I was poking around and started the sign up procedure on my PS3. This morning I woke to an email from them which backed up...

Read more →

Twitter 101

20th July 2012

This is a very quick post to explain something I see all the time – When people on twitter want to publicly mention another user, but start the tweet with a @username. If you start a tweet with '@username...', only people who follow both the person sending the tweet AND '@username' will see the tweet....

Read more →

FIGURE 1: www.tomalloyd.com

FIGURE 2: http://davidejones.com

FIGURE 3: http://tympanus.net/codrops

Blog

Beiträge, Tutorials, Tipps & Snippets rund um Webdesign und Social Media.

Das große Webdesign-Gewinnspiel!

http://blog.kulturbanause.de

CONFESIONES DESDE NARNIA / por JUAN A. PUNTOVÉ

Primeras citas

*La semana pasada, nuestro renovado
protagonista (@Juanapuntove) optó por dejar de
lado el sexo y buscar romance. También intentó
bajar de peso, pero mandó todo a la mierda y se
comió un pie de limón.*

L. es un tipo normal. Estudia, tiene vida,
totalmente promedio. Simpático, amoroso, buena
onda. Pero no engancho. Lo que sí me recuerda es
que Dios, hace tanto tiempo que no tenía una
primera cita, onda cita-cita, de yo intentando caer
bien y ser encantador y simpático, **onda no
querer sexo sino romance**. Es como WTF,
pero no importa. Por eso comienzo a salir, a
aceptar citas.

Primero son por Grindr, luego Scruff, luego por
gente que me recomienda otra gente, y bueno. Sigo

http://blog.japijane.cl

JEFFCR⦿FT
DESIGNER // CODER // WRITER // BOAT-ROCKER

I'm a digital product designer and developer in
Seattle, WA. I currently work with nGen Works,
and recently co-founded Lendle, a Kindle book
sharing service.

FILTER CONTENT

☐ Check-ins ☑ Blog entries ☑ Links ☑ Photos
☐ Dribbble shots ☐ Tweets

[FEED]

jQuery Controls: Responsive Design on Any Browser,
Any Platform, and Any Device
Powered by Fusion

PHOTO // 10.15.2012 // 10:52 PM // FLICKR

rip mca

⬈ Taken at Hula Hula, a Karaoke Bar in Seattle,
WA.

http://jeffcroft.com

The Modern
Gentleman

Blog für Männer und Mode.
Tipps zu Stil, Outfits und gutem
Geschmack.

Abonnierbar über RSS-Feed, Google+
oder Facebook.

---

10. September 2012

Sponsored Video:
Volvo You Inside
Project

Wenn man morgens auf dem Parkplatz
seiner Arbeitsstätte aus dem Auto steigt
und Kaugummis sowie Pfandflaschen
einem hinterherfallen, fragt man sich
sicherlich schon manchmal, ob das
nicht irgendwie als Charaktermerkmal
durchgehen würde. Beobachtet man andere Menschen, stellt man auch fest,
dass diesen ganz andere Dinge aus dem
Auto hinterherfallen. Ganz andere hin-

http://themoderngentleman.de

ORDEREDLIST **BLOG**
RESOURCES ABOUT

2012

OPEN SOURCE THEMES
FOR GITHUB — Apr 5

BACK TO THE BASICS — Feb 28

2011

ORDERED LIST ACQUIRED
BY GITHUB — Dec 5

SHARE PRESENTATIONS
WITHOUT THE MESS — Sep 26

FLARED BORDERS
WITH CSS — May 4

WELCOME MATT GRAHAM — May 2

GAUG.ES — Mar 1

DESIGN, FOCUS,
AND CONSTRAINTS — Feb 21

2011 REDESIGN — Jan 3

2010

FOUR — Dec 27

http://orderedlist.com/blog

A Delicious Valentine Dinner

02/16/2013
4 Responses

The February issue of Bon Appetit couldn't have been more timely. A feature on great pasta dishes just in time for Valentine's Day? Perfect. Of the seven delicious-sounding recipes in their feature, one caught both of our eyes for immediate consumption: the Orecchiette with Kale and Breadcrumbs. We planned it for our Valentine's dinner at home, complete with flowers and candles on the table. And it was so delicious, we both went back for seconds . . . and thirds!! There's a decent amount of prep (blanching kale, chopping it), but it is all completely worth it. If you're on the fence about kale, this will win you over. Spinach wouldn't be the same.

www.jasonanderin.com

Discover Paper

finding and sharing paper inspiration

Menu +   Search

Everyday Alphabet: Sculpture Today

http://discoverpaper.com

Rethinking WordPress Admin

January 3rd, 2013 | Posted in WordPress | 28 Comments and 0 Reactions

After having tackled customizing wp-admin with happytables, I've once again had the opportunity to go through the motions with an exciting project in a new vertical. The good news is that it's completely doable: The bad; it's time consuming, hacky and leaves a bad taste in your mouth (similar to doing responsive web design in a rush). [...]

Adaptive Content Images within WordPress

December 4th, 2012 | Posted in WordPress | 10 Comments and 0 Reactions

There are plenty of adaptive image solutions out there, but I needed one that understood the relevance of the content area, automatically created re-sized images for various breakpoints and minimized the download impact for end-users. Remember, images that are part of your theme should be solved through the theme files, my goal was to tackle any [...]

WordPress.com Verticals and the Future

November 30th, 2012 | Posted in WordPress | 8 Comments and 0 Reactions

Over the past few weeks, we've seen a number of

www.noeltock.com/blog

Kyle Haskins

▼   + Follow on Tumblr

Kyle is a user experience designer, visual designer, and front-end developer. He designs at Salesforce and previously built startups at SproutBox.

WTD: iOS 6 Commuting App

With all the criticism around iOS 6 maps, and specifically the outsourcing of transit data to routing apps, I think there is an opportunity to innovate on transit in iOS. While the iOS Google Maps app was great for navigating locations that you aren't that familiar - what if there was more attention paid to the transit that you use on a regular basis in your daily commute? Here's a quick sketch:

http://kylehaskins.com

Interview: Steve Matteson

There's a good chance you're intimately acquainted...

Our favorite tweets of the week: August 19, 2013 - August 25, 2013

Every week we...

Comics of the week #197

Every week we feature a set of comics created exclusively for WDD. The...

Deal of the week: Smashing Library

Smashing Magazine is one of the premium...

Andy Taylor

Jekyll Reading Time

11:32AM — Sunday April 7, 2013

Some of my posts now include an estimated reading time. I did this by taking the Liquid Filter, `number_of_words` and—based on a reading rate of 180wpm—used other Liquid filters to convert it to an approximate reading time. Here's the template code:

```
{{ page.content |
number_of_words | append:
'.0' | divided_by:180 |
append: 'min' }}
```

For this post, it will output: 1.6944444444444444min

Unfortunately the X.XXXmin figure is a bit verbose. I'd prefer a whole number, or at least X.Xmin. Without `append: '.0'` I was getting a whole number, but it wasn't rounded. So 1.9min would be 1min. Liquid provides more filters which could limit the figure to X characters, but they haven't been implemented by Jekyll.

A reading time on very short posts

THE PORTFOLIO OF
RYAN JOHNSON

Home   Blog   Shop   About

DONATELIFE PA

Automotive

I work very hard to feature lesser-known sites, but when it comes to mobile sites I have had to make a few exceptions. Automotive sites are one such exception. As it turns out, the automotive industry has really embraced the mobile web, and many brands have mobile-specific websites. I could actually fill a small book with samples in this area, but naturally I limited my selection to the small set you see here.

One thing that really strikes me about these mobile sites is how they truly cater to the mobile user. Sometimes it is hard to decide if a mobile site serves a different purpose than the desktop one, but here the difference is clear. A person on a desktop computer is likely researching cars and may even configure and begin the purchasing process. In contrast, a mobile user is most likely investigating specific cars and is perhaps even out taking test drives. I strongly suspect that very few people initiate the purchase of a new car via a brand's mobile website. Investigate mobile sites for auto brands and you will find this is true. The mobile sites are entirely geared toward quickly helping you learn about the cars and their options. Let's focus on a few to see what we can learn.

The Mercedes-Benz website **(FIGURE 1)** lists the models and starting prices all on one page. This brand has a lot of different vehicles ranging from $35,000 to $115,000. That is a large difference. By placing that information on the main list view, they help users more quickly find the car they are most likely to be interested in. This radically cuts down on the frustration of clicking on a car, looking for pricing, going back, etc. It is clearly focused on the user. I suspect it is tempting to first sell people on the cars and then give them pricing—an approach we frequently see on desktop sites. But Mercedes-Benz has effectively focused on the user and the results are much appreciated.

Another detail that many brands get right is showing you what each model looks like. To demonstrate this, look at the Kia website **(FIGURE 2)**. Here, they show a small image of each vehicle along with the model name. It is a simple detail, but it really helps. Without the images, someone less familiar with the brand would be perplexed at the options. Imagine having to click through to each to try to figure out what Kia has to offer. Instead, you can quickly scan the grid of images and see what might interest you. Again, it is a user-centered approach that makes it fun and easy to browse.

FIGURE 1: http://m.mbusa.com

FIGURE 2: www.kia.com

http://m.jeep.com/en/mobile

http://m.fiat.es

http://m.hb20.com.br

www.chevrolet.com

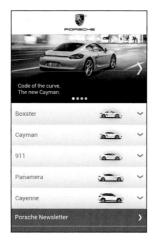

www.porsche.com/usa

www.cadillac.com

http://m.acura.com

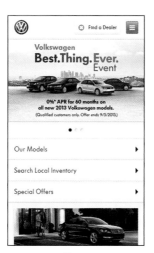

http://m.vw.com

http://m.scion.com

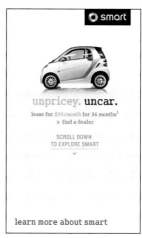

http://m.smartusa.com

www.honda.com Ⓜ

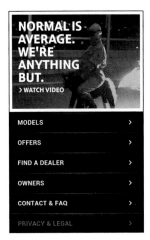

www.miniusa.com Ⓜ

www.ford.com/cars/mustang/2013 Ⓜ

www.dodge.com/en Ⓜ

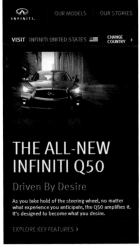

http://m.infiniti.com/us Ⓜ

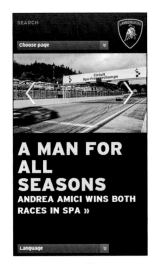

www.lamborghini.com Ⓜ

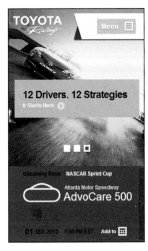

www.toyotaracing.com Ⓜ

http://mg.co.uk Ⓜ

Restaurants

In this chapter you will find a mix of brands you are familiar with and a few small restaurants that you're rather unlikely to know. In the previous chapter on Automotive sites, I highlighted that mobile sites often serve a different purpose, and we see a bit of this on restaurant sites as well. On these sites, the desktop and mobile sites essentially provide the exact same information, but the one nuance is that many mobile restaurant sites include a prominent location finder or mapping tool. Realizing that someone might be on your mobile site and trying to find the restaurant makes darn good sense, and placing a prominent link to this information is extremely helpful.

Just about every example here provides mapping services, but one that really does it well is PePe's Mi Mexico in Kentucky **(FIGURE 1)**. This restaurant has three locations and if you visit their site on a mobile device, the first thing you see is three jumbo-sized links. The links provide the full address and phone number. By providing all of this information up front, they make it simple for people on the go to locate or call them.

Many of the other examples take the approach you find on Mellow Mushroom **(FIGURE 2)**, where the first menu item on the site is a location finder. Though different sites use different wording, the strategy is frequently spotted. By placing it in the menu, it becomes a natural part of the navigation. But by placing it first on the list, it ensures it is rapidly located and used.

This approach is not universal though; take The Blue Lagoon Seafood Restaurant **(FIGURE 3)**, for example . Here, the home screen makes no mention of their location. I don't know this particular restaurant, but I do know that sometimes you simply don't need the info. If your restaurant is well known and is perhaps even a bit of landmark, you may not need to have the mapping option front and center. As always, the point is to carefully consider your project and website. There is almost always a reason or situation where it makes sense to break a trend or pattern.

FIGURE 1: www.
pepesfinemexicanrestaurant.com

FIGURE 2: http://mellowmushroom.
com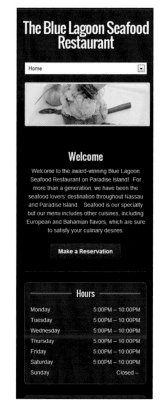

FIGURE 3: www.bluelagoonseafood.
com

http://fatdragon.com.au

http://bel50.com

www.bk.com

www.mcdonalds.com/us/en/home.html

OUR STORY

Italio is a modern Italian kitchen created with freshness in mind. Every meal is completely customizable and handcrafted in our open kitchen with only the finest and freshest ingredients. We believe in fast, flavorful meals. And we believe great food shouldn't break the bank.

Whether you take your time or take it to go, Italio invites you to enjoy a crisp salad, heaping pasta bowl or one of our legendary piadinas - thin, authentic Italian wraps filled with your choice of grilled entrée, delicate pasta, crisp vegetables, artisan cheese and house-made pesto and sauce.

http://italiokitchen.com

www.pizzaexpress.com

www.olivegarden.com

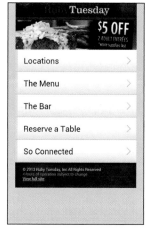

www.rubytuesday.com

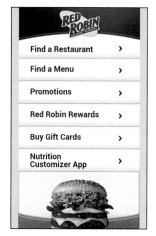

www.redrobin.com

Conferences

Conferences are big business, and it should come as no surprise that a lot of attention is put into their websites. This attention naturally flows into their mobile sites, as this is how attendees will likely interact with the events schedules while attending. In fact, this is one of the more vivid examples of how users may start on a desktop site but eventually turn to a mobile interface.

While in many areas of the mobile web minimalism is the focus, it seems that conference sites are much more intent on communicating the feel of the event. As such, you will find that this section features a nice range of stylized mobile sites. In fact, it is really one of the most stand-out sections of this book, in my opinion.

A fantastic example of this is the Ready to Inspire site **(FIGURE 1)**. This designer-centric event has a kitschy style that is fun, memorable and inviting. You may notice that the site seems to set the tone for the event long before it presents the user with a register button. In the screenshot here, you see a longer view than you would on an actual device. This strategy focuses on selling the event first, and then driving people to convert to paid attendees.

One of the most gorgeous examples here is the DISH conference **(FIGURE 2)**, a student design event. The style of the page is extremely elegant and gorgeous. It is clearly not as thematic as the Ready to Inspire site, and yet it sets a clear tone for the event. Even though it is for students, it feels first class and the design lets the user know what to expect. In this case you will notice that registration is front and center, and users are quickly directed there. My guess is that this is more of a local event and that attendance is cheaper than some bigger events. As such, quickly driving people to register is logical and plays into the idea that many people hitting the site will already be familiar with the event and are just ready to sign up.

Another interesting example is the Entrepreneurship Summit event site **(FIGURE 3)**. Here we find nothing in the way of thematic design and the layout is essentially built on typography. However, it does have an elegant style that resonates with a pragmatic audience. It is really interesting to me how a site's look and feel can so accurately be translated to the audience it needs to connect with. Even on the mobile web, there is more than enough room to tailor an experience to fit the site's specific niche.

FIGURE 1: https://2012.inspireconf.com

FIGURE 2: www.dishconference.com

FIGURE 3: www.summit.eship.cornell.edu

http://2012.full-frontal.org

Welcome to DrupalCon Munich 2012

DrupalCon is an international event that brings together the people who use, develop, design, and support the Drupal platform. More than just another trade show or industry conference, it's a shared experience that seeks to inspire and engage. DrupalCon Munich will feature dozens of curated sessions and panels from some of the most influential people and brightest minds within the Drupal community and beyond, as well as countless opportunities for networking, code sprints, informal conversations, and more. Whether you're new to the community, have been around a while, or are just curious to see what all the fuss is about - we have a place for you.

DrupalCon Munich final words

Sep 19 2012

Prost! To DrupalCon Munich

Thank you for helping us make DrupalCon Munich our biggest and most successful European conference yet! In the course of just a few days we had 3 amazing Keynotes, 102 sessions, 7 awesome pre-conference trainings, 3 days

http://munich2012.drupal.org Ⓜ

The 7th annual Future of Web Design proudly presents three days of cutting edge learning and inspiration. Join us for a day of in-depth workshops, followed by two action-packed conference

http://futureofwebdesign.com/london-2013 Ⓜ

http://conferenciarails.org Ⓜ

http://bdconf.com Ⓜ

Portland is a city of design and for design, unique in its approach to defining place, culture, and attitude. Design Week Portland celebrates design as our city's most promising cultural and economic resource. Our purpose is to explore process, craft, and practice across disciplines through our city's vibrant design programming.

Get Involved
Applications for events and open houses will launch this spring!

Contact Us
Say hello

Elsewhere
Twitter
Flickr
Tagboard
Vimeo

www.designweekportland.com

http://webdagene.no

http://dolectures.com

http://diglondon.ca

Coming Soon

Coming soon pages have become an important part of launching new websites. They allow you to build your marketing list, share a landing page with people and jump-start your placement in the search engines. While many people might put up less functional and less beautiful pages, some sites (like the ones presented here) take the time to craft responsive, beautiful and informative pages.

I really love examples that cut to the chase. Case in point is the Joiner coming soon page **(FIGURE 1)**. Here, the large six-word description sums it up. If you like the sounds of it, you can dig in for more details or simply sign up for their e-mail list. It proves that sometimes you don't need to overdo it: something small and to-the-point is all you need.

In other cases, such as the Editorially coming soon page **(FIGURE 2)**, the designers have included a bit more information. They still focus on building their marketing list. But after that, they have provided a fairly in-depth description of what they are working on. You will find a similar approach on the Dandy website **(FIGURE 3)**, where they again have the e-mail sign-up followed by an in-depth stream of the application, its functionality and its purpose.

Interestingly, in some cases, the landing page only hints at what is to come. Look at vnylst.com **(FIGURE 4)** for an example of such a case. Here, the subject matter is hinted at, but we have no idea what the site or its purpose will be. I suspect this is the difference between a pet project and a business that is pursuing funding. If you're just doing something for fun, you are perhaps content to have a less functional landing page. In contrast, if you are seeking funding, you will likely need to better communicate what you're up to and provide more detail before you launch.

FIGURE 1: www.joinerapp.com

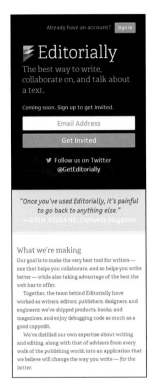

FIGURE 2: http://editorially.com

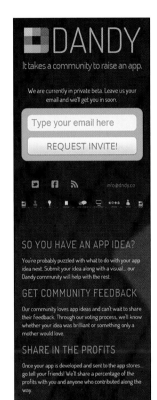

FIGURE 3: www.dndy.co

FIGURE 4: www.vnylst.com

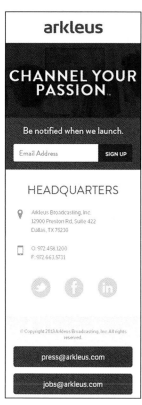

http://arkleus.com

www.blowapp.com.ar Ⓜ

www.threadcollection.com Ⓜ

http://herds.com/theherdapp Ⓜ

www.lookoutgaming.com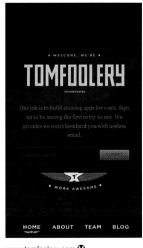

http://shoutapp.com.au

www.lokalhus.com

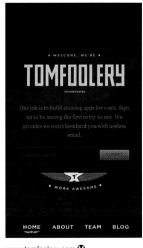

www.tomfoolery.com

Conclusion

Designing and building mobile and responsive sites presents a very real challenge to designers for many reasons. For example, the technical implications of everything you do are far more complicated, especially in the responsive world. In fact, the demands of responsive design are forcing many changes in the industry. A big side effect is that designers and developers are working together more and more. In fact the divide between these two groups is becoming greatly diminished. Agencies and companies that cling to these divides are finding it harder and harder to produce solid mobile work. While shops that embrace the change and work together well are excelling.

If I could leave you with one thought it would be to challenge you to embrace the other side and see what you can learn from them. The examples in this book should fill you with ideas, many of which will require your developer counter parts to implement. Befriend them, learn from them and work to be a bridge and I am certain you will find tremendous insights into designing and building mobile web sites.

Permissions

p. 222   http://evening-edition.com © 2012

p. 222   http://m.guardian.co.uk © 2012

p. 222   www.oggitreviso.it Multiways © 2012

p. 222   www.minnpost.com © 2012

p. 223   http://dontbeafuckingidiot.com/ © 2012

p. 223   http://thenextweb.com © 2012

p. 223   www.sbnation.com © 2012

p. 223   www.theonion.com © 2012

p. 226   http://m.gcu.edu © 2012

p. 226   http://m.harvard.edu © 2012

p. 226   http://m.umich.edu © 2012

p. 226   www.tuj.ac.jp © 2012

p. 227   http://asuonline.asu.edu © 2012

p. 227   www.lancs.ac.uk © 2012

p. 227   www.regent-college.edu © 2012

p. 227   www.wm.edu © 2012

p. 228   http://m.ncsu.edu © 2012

p. 228   http://m.uiowa.edu/home © 2012

p. 228   http://stories.cstudies.ubc.ca © 2012

p. 228   https://m.rit.edu/home © 2012

p. 229   http://arts.stanford.edu © 2012

p. 229   www.cambria.ac.uk © 2012

p. 229   www.luiss.edu © 2012

p. 229   www.mobap.edu © 2012

p. 231   www.barackobama.com © 2012

p. 231   www.democrats.org © 2012

p. 231   www.gop.com © 2012

p. 231   www.mittromney.com © 2012

p. 232   http://aids.gov © 2012

p. 232   http://moadoph.gov.au © 2012

p. 232   www.hannity.com © 2012

p. 232   www.hsgac.senate.gov © 2012

p. 233   http://apps.usa.gov © 2012

p. 233   m.ksdk.com © 2012

p. 233   www.ri.gov © 2012

p. 233   www.socialmediapoliticians.com © 2012

p. 235   http://tympanus.net/codrops © 2012

p. 235   http://davidejones.com David E Jones © 2012

p. 235   http://blog.kulturbanause.de kulturbanause® © 2012

p. 235   www.tomalloyd.com Tom A Lloyd © 2012

p. 236   http://blog.japijane.cl © 2012

p. 236   http://jeffcroft.com © 2012

p. 236   http://orderedlist.com/blog © 2012

p. 236   http://themoderngentleman.de © 2012

p. 237   http://discoverpaper.com © 2012

p. 237   http://kylehaskins.com © 2012

p. 237   www.jasonanderin.com © 2012

p. 237   www.noeltock.com/blog © 2012

p. 238   http://andytaylor.me © 2012

p. 238   http://mmcneil.com © 2012

p. 238   http://ryjohnson.com © 2012

p. 238   www.webdesignerdepot.com © 2012

p. 240   http://m.fiat.es © 2012

p. 240   http://m.jeep.com/en/mobile © 2012

p. 240   http://m.mbusa.com © 2012

p. 240   www.kia.com © 2012

p. 241   http://m.acura.com © 2012

p. 241   http://m.hb20.com.br © 2012

p. 241   http://m.scion.com © 2012

p. 241   http://m.smartusa.com © 2012

p. 241   http://m.vw.com © 2012

p. 241   www.cadillac.com © 2012

More Great Titles from HOW Books

The Designer's Web Handbook | Patrick McNeil

Too many designers are unaware of the differences they'll face when designing for the web. Things like efficient navigation and building for easy updates or changes may be neglected in the planning process. This book will help you avoid making those costly mistakes so that your designs work the way you want them to.

Above the Fold | Brian Miller

A different kind of web design book, *Above the Fold* is not about timely design or technology trends. Instead, you'll learn about the timeless fundamentals of effective communication within the context of web design. You'll gain a deeper understanding of the web design considerations including design, typography, planning, usability and business value.

The Strategic Web Designer | Christopher Butler

In *The Strategic Web Designer,* you'll learn how to think about the web and lead web projects from the critical inception phase through the ongoing nurturing process every website needs. This indispensible guide provides a comprehensively informed point of view on the web that enables you to guide a web project intentionally, rather than reactively.

 Find these books and many others at MyDesignShop.com or your local bookstore.